FACE TO FACE
THE THEOLOGY OF THE ICON

Also published by Gracewing

Beauty, Spirit, Matter: Icons in the Modern World
Festal Icons
Techniques of Icon and Wall Painting

Face to Face

THE THEOLOGY OF THE ICON

Aidan Hart

GRACEWING

First published in England in 2025
by
Gracewing
2 Southern Avenue
Leominster
Herefordshire HR6 0QF
United Kingdom
www.gracewing.co.uk

All rights reserved

No part of this publication may be reproduced, stored in a retrieval system, or transmitted in any form or by any means, electronic, mechanical, photocopying, recording or otherwise, without the written permission of the publisher.

© 2025, Aidan Hart

The rights of Aidan Hart to be identified as the author of this work have been asserted in accordance with the Copyright, Designs and Patents Act 1988.

The publishers have no responsibility for the persistence or accuracy of URLs for websites referred to in this publication, and do not guarantee that any content on such websites is, or will remain, accurate or appropriate.

ISBN 978 085244 710 9

Cover image: Mother of God Glycophilousa (Sweetly Kissing), by Aidan Hart

Cover design by Bernardita Peña Hurtado

Typeset by Word and Page, Chester, UK

Contents

Acknowledgements	vi
Introduction	1
1. What is an Icon?	5
2. Iconoclasm in Byzantium	19
3. The Orthodox Response to Iconoclasm	25
4. Icons and Imageless Prayer	43
5. The Use of Icons	47
6. Icon Form and Theology	53
7. Iconography beyond Traditionally Orthodox Countries	71
8. The Return of the Icon to Western Europe	83
Bibliography	95

Acknowledgements

This publication is adapted for the book format from my article, 'The Theology of the Icon', written for the online St Andrew's Encyclopaedia of Theology (https://www.saet.ac.uk/). It was felt that a printed version was a necessary partner to the online version, and indeed the editors of SAET encourage such printing of its articles. And so, my hearty thanks to its principal editor, Dr Brendan Wolfe, both for giving permission and for his guiding forward the whole SAET project. Many thanks also to the John Templeton Foundation, which funded the articles.

My appreciation also goes to Clive Tolley, my eagle-eyed copy-editor. The incisiveness of his mind in noticing referencing errors and lapses in logic matches the sharpness of the Japanese *gyuto* knife, though any remaining errors remain my own responsibility. Finally, my thanks to Tom Longford of Gracewing Publishers, who many years ago took the risk of publishing my first book, a large and bountifully illustrated work.

Scriptural texts are cited from the New Revised Standard Version, Anglicized.

Introduction

'I am not a church-goer, but these icons speak to me. I don't understand why, but they touch my heart.' So often have I heard this response from members of the general public. Icons speak the language of the spirit. 'Deep calls to deep', as the Psalmist says (Psalm 42.7). The recognition of their importance is evidenced by the many exhibitions that leading museums have hosted over the past few decades.

Although made primarily for use in the Orthodox Church's worship, the icon is also being widely revived in Catholic and Anglican churches. This renewed appreciation of the sacred image now needs to be deepened by its marriage to the word of Scripture, hymnography, and the Church Fathers. Only in this way can the icon's theological depth be better understood.

It might be asked why a new book on the theology of the icon is needed when we already have the classic works by Leonid Ouspensky, *The Theology of the Icon* and *The Meaning of Icons*. First, this work is more compact and as such is an easier-to-read introduction to the icon. It attempts to cover all the major areas of the icon's theology with the precision required of an encyclopaedia, while offering extensive references for those who wish to read further. We have retained the system of subheadings found in the online version to make it easier for the reader to locate a particular subject.

Second, this book includes recent scholarship, referencing, for example, the refreshingly holistic visions of the three influential scholars Katherine Marsengill, Bissera Pentcheva, and Cornelia Tsakiridou.

Third, I have tried to avoid the anti-Western polemic that has influenced some writers on the icon. This book covers, for example, the important influence of the icon on the founding abstract artists of the early twentieth century. As a professional iconographer in the West for over forty years and a teacher of the art, I also believe it is important that the tradition learns from all that is good in Western European art, drawing inspiration, for example, from the rich seams of Anglo-Saxon and Romanesque liturgical art.

The Christian icon—literally 'image' in Greek—has been part of liturgical worship from the early centuries of the Christian era, and sometimes also a subject of theological debate. On the one hand, icons have been described by iconodules or iconophiles (those defending icons and their veneration) as theology in material form and as doors between heaven and earth. They have asserted that images of Christ affirm the reality of God's enfleshment in Christ: Christ God can be depicted because he has become a visible human. They defended icons of saints as affir-

Introduction

mations of the purpose of the Incarnation, namely, to bring people into union with God—a process of deification or *theosis*, as this union is also named. On the other hand, those opposed to images—iconoclasts ('icon smashers') or iconophobes (those averse to or 'afraid' of icons)—have condemned them as idols or, at best, as impediments to a relationship with God.

Extant images of Christ and the saints found on catacomb walls date certainly from the early third century, and possibly from as early as the late second century (Finney 1994: 146). For two periods during the eighth and ninth centuries, theological debate erupted within the Eastern Roman Empire (generally referred to as Byzantium from the nineteenth century) between iconoclasts and iconodules. The dispute was eventually won in favour of icons. Thereafter, sacred imagery was firmly established as an integral part of Christian liturgy, though with East and West placing different emphases on their role.

From around the mid-thirteenth century, liturgical art in the Catholic West gradually became more naturalistic, in line with theological and philosophical changes. The picture was further complicated with the rise of Protestant iconoclasm from the sixteenth century. In the meantime, traditional iconography, though sometimes stylistically influenced by these currents, continued in the Orthodox Church with far less change, hence the current association of iconography primarily with Orthodoxy. In the early twentieth century, this Orthodox icon tradition was reintroduced to the Western European world, and then internationally, to stimulate fresh research and discussion about the relationship between the form and function of Christian iconography.

Icons are made primarily for liturgical use, be they painted, carved, or made of metal, mosaic, or fabric. This use has profoundly influenced their form. The theological significance of this form has inspired much study over the past century, challenging as it does a rationalistic and anthropocentric world view. Though made for liturgical use, icons have had a profound impact beyond church walls, such as in mission, and in offering a theological paradigm for addressing contemporary issues such as ecology, the nature of the human person, art, and the relationship between tradition and innovation.

— 1 —

What is an Icon?

The word 'icon' is derived from the Greek term *eikon*, meaning primarily 'likeness' and hence 'image'. This book uses the term to refer above all to Christian images, and concentrates on that form of Christian imagery now most associated with the word icon, namely, the iconography of the Eastern Orthodox Church. However, it also includes Western liturgical art of the first twelve centuries or so, whose stylistic similarities with Eastern Christian iconography indicate that it broadly shared the same vision of the world. Although there were differences in emphasis, before the rise of the Gothic style the iconography of Western Christendom broadly followed the same trajectory as that of the Church in the Eastern Roman empire, both in being primarily liturgical in function and in their degree of stylistic abstraction. Gothic art, which gradually eclipsed the Romanesque from the mid-twelfth century, gave more emphasis to expressive emotion and closer naturalistic rendition, the latter trend accelerating during the Italian Renaissance.

Although for most people the word icon means painted panel icons, this book applies the term to sacred Christian images in whatever medium, as did the Second Council of Nicaea (787), where the definition of its sixth session declared that 'venerable and holy icons—made of colours, pebbles [i.e. mosaic] or any other material that is fit—may be set in the holy churches of God, on holy utensils and vestments, on walls and boards, in houses and in streets' (Sahas 1986: 179).

The term *eikon* can, however, refer to a conceptual image as well as to a physical image, and as such correlates with perception and imagination. A major defender of icons, St John of Damascus (*c.* 675–749), includes this meaning in his hierarchy of icons, as the 'ideas' or 'paradigms' of creation, present in God before he actualized them in physical form (see below).

An image, whilst being like its prototype, is also unlike it—otherwise it would be the prototype. In the context of Christian images of holy persons, it is therefore necessary to clarify from the beginning what exactly material images do and do not represent. An icon of a holy person is connected to its subject through likeness to their unique person (*hypostasis* or *prosopon* in Greek patristic theology)—John, Paul, Mary, or whoever—and not through likeness to their generic nature as human beings (*physis* in Patristic Greek), which is of a different order from their person (for a fuller treatment of hypostasis, see pp. 26–30). The nature (or constitution) of a painted panel icon, for example, remains inanimate wood and pigment, while the nature of the saint whom it depicts is that of a human of flesh and blood and

What is an Icon?

soul united to God. When Orthodox Christians kiss an icon, they are therefore addressing the person whose likeness is depicted on the image and not the image in and of itself.

THE PURPOSE OF ICONS

Icons can be appreciated fully only when understood within three contexts: first, icons are liturgical, made to be part of Christian worship; second, they manifest God's incarnation in matter, both in creation in general and in the incarnation of God in Christ in particular; third, icons manifest the fruit of this incarnation, which is the deification of human persons within the Body of Christ. In the words of St Athanasius the Great in his *On the Incarnation of the Word* 54.3: 'God became human that we might become divine' (author's translation; cf. Athanasius 2011: 167). Concordant with this deification is the transfiguration of the whole cosmos, much as Christ's garment was transfigured along with his body.

In whatever medium they are made, icons function as an integral part of the Orthodox Church's worship, both within the church building and in homes and public places. They are best understood as the visual element of a multi-sensual act of people's worship of God and of God's self-revelation to people. Icons are kissed as a means of greeting those depicted thereon. They are used in processions, prayed in front of, worn, placed on sacred vessels, and even literally used as doors in the case of the Beautiful Gates (also called Royal Doors) found in the centre of the icon screen that demarcates the sanctuary from the nave. When covering walls with frescos or mosaics, one aim is to create a lively sense that worship on earth participates in worship in heaven, a visual manifestation of the 'communion of the saints' described in the book of Hebrews:

> But you have come to Mount Zion and to the city of the living God, the heavenly Jerusalem, and to innumerable angels in festal gathering, and to the assembly of the firstborn who are enrolled in heaven, and to God the judge of all, and to the spirits of the righteous made perfect, and to Jesus …
>
> (Heb 12:22–4a)

These ritual functions profoundly affect the icon's aesthetic form, its 'style'. These forms legitimately vary from culture to culture and epoch to epoch, as at Pentecost when the Apostles declared the same truths in different tongues. However, amidst this cultural diversity of style, icons preserve features that immediately identify them as icons rather than as art with a religious theme. These aesthetic forms and their functions are discussed in more detail below, but suffice it to say here that they reflect and embody a vision of the world transfigured.

Cornelia Tsakiridou, in her book *Icons in Time, Persons in Eternity* (2013), uses the Greek word *enargeia* (a term used for 'vividness' in rhetorical discourse, from *arges*, 'bright'; not to be confused with *ener-*

geia or 'energy') to describe how the icon's aesthetics embody what it depicts, and directly impress on the viewer the beauty of truth. This term *enargeia* denotes the capacity of an artwork to evoke through aesthetic means its subject as though present. According to Tsakiridou: '*Enargeia* is *hypostatic*. We see a face in the act of *existing* and *actualizing* its austerity, gentleness, authority, etc.' (2013: 54). Icons, therefore, aim to bring people into the presence of the saints depicted, rather than merely offering an aesthetic experience or simply providing information about them.

While the aesthetic form of icons has undoubtedly been affected by their being images of saints destined for devotional use rather than viewed as secular portraits, Katherine Marsengill has called for a more nuanced approach that also considers icons as a Christianized continuation of antique portraiture. In her work *Portraits and Icons* (2013), she calls for a 'new approach […] that maintains the icon as dependent upon the genre of the portrait, while recognizing in many types of Byzantine portraiture an ongoing dialogue, with portraits and icons mutually defining one another' (2013: 295–6).

Just as icons of people seek actualization through the representations' *enargeia*, icons of sacred events aim to engage the faithful in these events as a divine activity; while such events occurred at a particular time in the past, their effects are not limited in time. This is possible because of a theological distinction between two types of time, often denoted by the Greek words *chronos* and *kairos*. *Chronos* signifies sequential time and therefore connotes its fleeting quality. It is quantitative. This is to be distinguished from *kairos*, which is qualitative and denotes divine action at the right time. *Chronos* implies the limits of created time, whereas *kairos* indicates God opening created time to eternity, directing it towards its *telos* or end. We can say that *kairos* is therefore incarnational, denoting God's self-limitation within the 'swaddling bands' of created time in order to open cyclical and enclosed time into eternity. Then, 'creation itself will be set free from its bondage to decay and will obtain the freedom of the glory of the children of God' (Rom 8.21).

The effects of divine action within *chronos*, therefore, flow both forwards and backwards in time. This explains the frequent use of the word 'today' in Orthodox hymns:

> Today Christ has come to be baptized
> in the Jordan. …
> Today is salvation come into the world,
> for Christ is risen.

This 'kairotic' role of icons explains some of its forms. In Annunciation icons, for example, the Virgin is often shown looking out at the viewer, as though saying: 'Do you also wish to have Christ born in you today?'

Such personalism introduces another function of icons: they help keep the Christian faith as a relation of persons and so help to preserve it from degradation into a mere philosophical or moral system. Above all, icons are images of faces, and therefore

What is an Icon?

of persons. The word for face is synonymous with the word for person in both the Greek term *prosopon* and the Latin *persona*. When visitors enter a church full of images of saints and angels, they can be in no doubt that membership of the Church is membership in a family, and a family that encompasses those in heaven as well as those on earth.

SCRIPTURE AND IMAGES

Setting aside for a moment the hand-crafted icon, the concept of image runs throughout the Scriptures. It begins with the divine words: 'Let us make humankind in our image' (Gen 1:26), continues through to the Tent of Meeting, whose pattern was divinely revealed to Moses (Ex 25–7), and culminates in the Christology expounded in the New Testament of 'Christ, who is the image of God' (2 Cor 4:4).

The strict directives God gave to Moses about how to build the Tent of Meeting point to this structure's iconographic status. As the writer to the Hebrews stated:

> They offer worship in a sanctuary that is a sketch and shadow of the heavenly one; for Moses, when he was about to erect the tent, was warned, 'See that you make everything according to the pattern that was shown you on the mountain'.
>
> (Heb 8:5)

The Tent of Meeting was an icon of heavenly worship (hence the cherubim) and was full of types or prefigurations of Christ, such as the Ark of the Covenant. Since only God knew the heavenly prototype, only he could know how to represent it in this Tent of Meeting.

From this it is clear that God willed the Israelites to be a people of the material image as much as of the written word. Here it is important to distinguish between images—which, as shown above, were allowed in the Old Testament—and idols, which were not. An idol is a created entity treated as though it were God, while valid images, such as those ordained by God for the Israelites, are precisely images, reflections, or impresses of their prototypes and are not the prototypes themselves.

THE ONTOLOGY OF IMAGE: IMAGE HIERARCHY IN ST JOHN OF DAMASCUS

Before proceeding to the liturgical icon, it is helpful to situate it within the broader reality of an image's ontology, its place within the whole of creation, and indeed, within the Holy Trinity itself.

In his first treatise *On the Divine Images*, John of Damascus (c. 675–749) explains how the Scriptures show how image is ontological both to creation and to the Creator himself. John outlines five orders of images not made by human craft, beginning with the highest icon: the Second Person of the Trinity. Referring to the words of Paul that the Son is 'the image (*eikon*) of the invisible God' (Col 1:15), he writes:

> The Son is a living, natural and undeviating Image of the Father, bearing in himself the whole

What is an Icon?

> Father, equal to him in every respect, differing only in being caused; for the Father is not from the Son, but the Son from the Father.
>
> (*On the Divine Images* 1.9–13; 2003: 25)

John is saying that image is an eternal characteristic in the Holy Trinity, for the Son is the likeness of the Father according to their shared and identical divine nature. What John means by the Son being the 'natural' image of the Father is that he is of the same essence or nature as the Father. He is 'true God from true God', as the Nicene Creed affirms. While humans can become 'participants in the divine nature' by the will of God (2 Pet 1:4), the Son is divine by nature.

Equally importantly, the Son is not the Father, being distinct in person. The Son is begotten, while the Father is the begetter. This first level of the icon is illustrated by the foremost among the images of Christ, the icon 'Not Made by Human Hands' (*Acheiropoietos* in Greek), also called the Mandilion (Greek for napkin). The legend says that Christ pressed a cloth to his face and miraculously imprinted his image upon it. The significance of this icon and its title is primarily theological. Christ's person is the eternal Logos, 'begotten not made', and is therefore not made by human hands or conception. The *Acheiropoietos* icon is therefore taken as the first depiction of Christ, for not only is the cloth image not made by human hands, but Christ's person, which is what it depicts, is also not made by human agency. Nor is Christ made by God the Father, but is begotten before all ages of the Father. By the time of John of Damascus, the Mandilion story was taken as historical fact. John refers to it in *On the Divine Images* 1.33: Jesus 'took a strip of cloth and lifted it to his face, marking it with his own form. The cloth survives to this day' (2003: 41).

In *On the Divine Images* 1.10 John identifies the second form of icon in his hierarchy as the pre-existent 'images and paradigms' within God of things that, from our perspective within created time, God will later bring into existence (2003: 25). This relates to what Paul calls God's 'eternal purpose that he has carried out in Christ Jesus our Lord' (Eph 3:11). These purposes of things yet to come existed in God before all the ages and are therefore beyond the category of created time. This concept of ideas in God's mind is suggested by the phrase 'let us' in the first chapter of Genesis, as though the persons of the Trinity were ruminating on the idea before actually creating: 'Then God said, "Let us make humankind in our image, according to our likeness"' (Gen 1:26).

The third level of image (*On the Divine Images* 1.11; 2003: 26) are those forms which God has provided to offer mankind a 'dim understanding' of invisible and formless things. This is what Paul refers to in Rom 1:20 when he writes how God's 'eternal power and divine nature, invisible though they are, have been understood and seen through the things he has made'. All creation is therefore an icon of God's power and divinity. Unlike the two previous types of image, this and the following ones are created by God in time.

The fourth level suggested by John (*On the Divine Images* 1.12; 2003: 27) concerns typological images. These are people, objects, or events from the Old Testament that foreshadow things to come. The Ark of the Covenant, as an example, is an image of the Virgin Mary, and the brazen serpent on a pole an image of the crucifixion.

The fifth type of image (*On the Divine Images* 1.13; 2003: 27) recalls things that have already happened. These may be words written in books or may be objects. John gives as an example the jar of manna kept in the Ark of the Covenant to remind the Israelites that God fed them when they were in the wilderness.

Although not in his list of icons, John clearly also understands humanity to be an icon of God, something that is reflected in Orthodox church services when the priest censes the congregation as well as the icons. Mankind's iconographic nature is stated unambiguously in Gen 1:26: 'Let us make humankind in our image', image being *eikon* in the Septuagint, the translation of the Old Testament used by most of the Greek-speaking Christian community at the time of Christ and then by the early Church.

An important note here is that later Church Fathers saw the plural statement 'let us' as a hint of the Holy Trinity. This implies that human persons are created in the Trinity's image not as isolated individuals but as beings in relationship, in communion. This observation helps explain the presence of images of saints and angels in churches, for they affirm this communal nature of persons made in the Trinity's image.

THE SECOND COMMANDMENT

Those opposed to icons usually quote the Second Commandment as proof that icons contravene the Scriptures:

> 'You shall not make for yourself an idol, whether in the form of anything that is in heaven above, or that is on the earth beneath, or that is in the water under the earth.'
>
> (Ex 20:4; Deut 5:7–9)

In the Septuagint the term translated as 'idol' is *eidolon*, and 'likeness' is *homoioma*, which also means 'form'. Yet in the very same book of Exodus God instructs Moses to have curtains made 'with cherubim skilfully worked into them' (Ex 26:1), and two cherubim of hammered gold to be placed at the ends of the Mercy Seat on the Ark of the Covenant (Ex 25:22). God later commanded Moses to make an image of a serpent, so that people bitten by a snake could look towards this bronze image and be healed (Num 21:6–9). Clearly, the commandment against making idols was not against making images as such.

The Church Fathers give various reasons why New Testament icons of Christ do not contravene this commandment. The chief is that, by becoming flesh, the Second Person of the Trinity became visible

What is an Icon?

and therefore depictable. The words of the Second Council of Nicaea, also called the Seventh Ecumenical Council, teach the following: 'One of these traditions [of the Church] is the making of iconographic representations […] for the purpose of ascertaining the incarnation of the Word of God, which was real, not imaginary, and for being of equal benefit to us as the Gospel narrative' (Sahas 1986: 178–9).

It is then reasonable to ask why images of 'things on earth below' were prohibited, even of holy people, since they were visible and therefore technically depictable. St John of Damascus first offers a pragmatic reason, suggesting that, because of the weakness of mankind before the descent of the Holy Spirit, it would have been easy for the Israelites to worship images of creatures, as did the surrounding idolaters, and as indeed they themselves did with the golden calf (Ex 32:1–35):

> It was, therefore, for the Jews, on account of their sliding into idolatry, that these things [i.e. the commandments against making images] were ordained by law.
>
> *(On the Divine Images* 1.8; 2003: 24)

A further, more theological, reason offered by John of Damascus is related to the corruption that ruled before Christ's coming and the separation of the living and the dead this entailed. Icons of people in the New Covenant are of people who are alive in heaven and in their glorified state thanks to Christ 'trampling down death by death' (as the Easter troparion states) and having raised human nature at his Resurrection (although mankind's full glorification is not until the Parousia and the bodily resurrection that accompanied it). By contrast, St John of Damascus points out that before the coming of Christ 'Israel neither set up temples in the name of human beings nor celebrated the memorials of any human', as Christians were later to do:

> for human nature was still under the curse and death was condemnation ... but now, since the divinity has been united to our nature, as a kind of lifegiving and saving medicine, our nature has been glorified and its very elements changed into incorruption. Therefore the death of the saints is celebrated and temples raised for them and images engraved.
> (*On the Divine Images* 2.10; 2003: 67, 68)

He appears to be saying that images of humans would have been premature before Christ's death and resurrection, and the descent of the Holy Spirit at Pentecost. This may explain why it was acceptable for Moses, by God's command, to make an image of two cherubim (Ex 25:18–20), since not being corrupted by the Fall the cherubim remained in their glorious state. One could also add that this image of cherubim was unlikely to incite idolatry since, residing in the Holy of Holies, only the High Priest ever saw them, and even then just once a year at Passover.

2

Iconoclasm in Byzantium

ICONS BEFORE EIGHTH-CENTURY ICONOCLASM

It is clear both from extant imagery and written sources that icons existed from at least the beginning of the third century. The oldest surviving images are wall paintings from the catacombs, such as those of Domitilla and the Capella Greca in the catacombs of Priscilla, which date certainly from the early third century, but may be earlier, from the end of the second century (Spier 2009: 1–13). The oldest extant church with figurative images is the house church at Dura-Europos in Syria, dated to 235 (Peppard 2016).

Regarding literary evidence, the Church historian Eusebius seems to have been ambiguous about Christian imagery. He nevertheless does acknowledge in his *History of the Church* (7.18), written between 312 and 324, that 'the features of [Christ's] apostles Paul and Peter, and indeed of Christ himself, have been preserved in coloured portraits which I have examined' (Eusebius 1965: 302). Earlier still, Clement of Alexandria (c.150–215) in his *Paedagogus* III.59.2 wrote that Christians ought to use only those seal rings that bear images of things that could be given a Christian symbolic meaning, and cites as examples a dove, fish, ships, lyres, anchors, or fishermen.

Apart from the Mandilion already mentioned, pious tradition has the Evangelist Luke painting the first icon of the Virgin Mary (see Boeckl 2019). The oldest extant reference to this is an early-sixth-century text by the historian Theodorus Anagnostes (Lector). He writes that the widowed Empress Aelia Eudocia sent the image of the Mother of God, painted by the Evangelist Luke, from Palestine to her sister Pulcheria, the wife of Emperor Marcian in Constantinople.

Soon after his Edict of Milan (313) to legalize Christianity across the whole empire, Emperor Constantine funded many churches and had them decorated with mosaics, though it is uncertain how many of these were figurative. One of the oldest extant Christian figurative mosaics in Rome, albeit heavily restored in the sixteenth century, is that of Santa Pudenziana's apse, dated variously to between 384 and 417.

Putting aside the liturgical, theological, or pedagogical reasons for making and using these images, it is clear from the high volume of Christian imagery produced from the early fourth century onwards that the dominant belief within Christendom was that sacred images should be made, valued, and used.

Some opposition to images did exist during this time, but it was limited before the outbreak of iconoclasm. Among many early Christian writers who appear at times to express negative opinions about images, such as Eusebius, scholars debate whether they were outright opponents of images *per se*, or merely of their abuse (for an assessment, see Bigham 2004). Writing before the outbreak of official iconoclasm in 727, Patriarch Germanus I of Constantinople reprimanded two iconoclast bishops, Constantine of Nacoleia in Phrygia and Thomas of Claudiopolis, saying that because of their iconoclast tendencies 'whole towns and multitudes of people are in considerable agitation over this matter' (Mango 1977: 1). Another bishop opposed to (or at least wary of) images was Theodosius of Ephesus (in office c. 729–54). Iconoclasts asserted that St Epiphanius of Salamis (c. 310–403) was against images in principle, but there is debate whether some of the passages attributed to him are spurious, and also whether passages commonly quoted as proof of his iconophobia express his opposition to icons in principle or merely to cases of abuse. For an appraisal of Epiphanius' writings on icons, see Bigham 2008.

A BACKGROUND TO BYZANTINE ICONOCLASM

Iconoclasm, as an imperial policy of the Eastern Roman Empire, had two phases. The first was initiated by Emperor Leo III the Isaurian in 726–7 and ran until 787. The second phase, probably milder, extended from 814 until the death of the iconoclast Emperor Theophilus in 842. In between these, the Empress Irene called the Second Council of Nicaea in 787. This defined what became the official Church view in favour of having and venerating images of Christ and the saints.

Official iconoclasm finally ended in 843 when the regent Empress Theodora II—appointed by her husband before his death to rule on behalf of their two-year-old son Michael III—and the court official Theoctistus installed the iconophile Methodius I as Patriarch of Constantinople. This restoration of icons was celebrated by a triumphant procession through Constantinople to the church of Hagia Sophia and the celebration of the liturgy, an event commemorated by the modern Orthodox Church as the Triumph of Orthodoxy on the first Sunday of Great Lent. Through this yearly celebration, with its theological hymns and the reading of the Council's doctrinal declaration, the theology of the icon has been made to permeate not only the more erudite circles of the Church but also, repeatedly and directly, all ranks of the laity.

The reasons for the iconoclast policy are multiple, some theological and some political. It does seem that many Byzantines believed that their numerous defeats by the iconoclastic Muslim armies were due to God's displeasure at the Christian empire condoning images. Here we shall consider only the theological elements of the debate. Although the consequences of iconoclasm for those living at the time are regrettable, the controversy did serve to compel the Church, particularly that of the Eastern Empire to which this iconoclasm was limited, to delve more deeply into the theology of the image than it might otherwise have done.

Iconoclasm in Byzantium

TENETS OF ICONOCLASM

Since most of the extant records of iconoclast doctrine are provided by iconodules, a fair and full representation of iconoclast thinking is not guaranteed. However, three iconoclast beliefs are clear from the iconodules' answers to their opponents. First, they believed icons to be idols and therefore a contravention of the Second Commandment; second, they considered the veneration of icons a sign of idolatry, supposing people to be worshipping the image itself and not the person depicted; third, they considered icons an innovation, an import from paganism with no support from Church tradition.

The iconoclasts provided a summary of their theological defence in the acts of their Council of Hiereia, which met in 754. The statements of this council are found dispersed throughout the text of the subsequent iconodule Second Council of Nicaea (Nicaea II; Sahas 1986). The Hiereia Council had been called by the most vigorous of the iconoclast emperors, Constantine V (ruled 741–75), the son of Leo III, to give his views on Church approbation. Hiereia's edicts were soon rejected by the Church: first in the Lateran Council of 769 and then in Nicaea II. Hiereia was repudiated not only because of its teachings but also because not one of the patriarchates was represented, namely those of Rome, Jerusalem, Antioch, Alexandria, or Constantinople, although this last city had no patriarch at the time of the council.

The chief assumption that underpinned all the iconoclasts' other views on images is described by the epitome of the iconoclastic Hiereia acts as follows:

> For [the painter] has made an icon which he has called 'Christ'. But 'Christ' is the name [indicative] of God as well as man. Consequently, along with describing created flesh, he has either circumscribed the uncircumscribable character of the Godhead, according to what has seemed good to his own worthlessness, or he has confused that unconfused union, falling into the iniquity of confusion. Thus, in two ways, with the circumscription and the confusion, he has blasphemed the Godhead.
>
> (Sahas 1986: 83)

As is discussed next, iconodules pointed out that this statement was inherently contradictory and in error.

— 3 —

The Orthodox Response to Iconoclasm

As well as the Second Council of Nicaea itself and the writings of John of Damascus, the other chief exponents of the iconodule position were St Germanus I of Constantinople (c. 634–733/740), St Theodore the Studite (759–826), and St Nicephorus I of Constantinople (c. 758–828).

Though most of Germanus' writings were destroyed by Leo III, some remain, including his *Three Dogmatic Epistles on the Iconoclasts*, letters written to Bishop John of Synada just before the outbreak of iconoclasm, to Bishop Constantine of Nacaleia, and to Bishop Thomas of Claudiopolis (*Concilium Nicaenum* II, Actio IV. Mansi 13, 100B–128A).

In 730, soon after the outbreak of iconoclasm under Emperor Leo III, John of Damascus began to write his three treatises in defence of icons, collectively known as *The Defence against those who attack the Holy Image*s. Ironically, it was because he lived in an area conquered by aniconic Muslims (in Mar Saba Monastery near Jerusalem) that he could write freely, the enforcers of Byzantine iconoclasm not being able to reach him.

Theodore the Studite wrote *On the Holy Icons* during the second phase of iconoclasm. This work consists of three refutations of the iconoclasts. Theodore reiterated John of Damascus' thinking but more fully developed the icon's relation to Christology.

Nicephorus I of Constantinople's works (not yet translated into English, but see Alexander 1958, and for French see Bigham 2017) are less polemical than those of the previous three writers. He was patriarch from 806 to 815, and thus most of his patriarchate fell between the first and second iconoclasms. He was deposed in 815 by the iconoclastic synod at Constantinople and exiled to a monastery near Chalcedon. It was there in 817 that he wrote his major work in defence of icons, *Apologeticus Major* ('Major Apology').

Both the Eastern Orthodox and the Roman Catholic Churches consider the theology of these four saints as normative. We will now consider the works of John, Theodore, and the Acts of Nicaea II in more detail.

NATURE AND PERSON

The theological basis of the Orthodox Church's response to the Hiereia declarations of the iconoclasts could be summarized in one sentence by Theodore the Studite:

> When anyone is portrayed, it is not the nature but the hypostasis which is portrayed.
>
> (Theodore, *On the Holy Icons* 3.34; 1981: 90)

In other words, the central mistake of the iconoclasts was to think that icons attempted to depict the *natures* of holy persons rather than their *persons* or hypostasis—Christ, Peter, Paul, or whoever.

What Theodore means by hypostasis and nature requires explanation. By the time of the Council of Chalcedon (451), the Greek terms *hypostasis* and *physis* (nature)—as well as the latter's virtual equivalent, *ousia* (variously translated as essence or substance)—had assumed a technical meaning in orthodox theology. One way of distinguishing the two terms is to say that the term *physis*/nature describes *what* an entity is, while hypostasis describes *how* it is that identity. Hypostasis is therefore an identity's distinctive mode of being that identifies it as the particular being that it is. For example, in *Letter* 38, written to his younger brother Gregory, Basil of Caesarea (329–379) described nature or essence as signifying the general, such as the human nature that all people hold in common, while the term hypostasis refers to the particular, to each person in the case of humans.

Understood in this generalized way, the term hypostasis can be applied to animals as well as to persons—to denote a particular lion, for example, as distinct from the lion species. However, in theological discourse, the term hypostasis is usually used in respect of the three persons of the Holy Trinity: Father, Son, and Holy Spirit. In Greek theology, the term *prosopon* was also used interchangeably with hypostasis when referring to persons. For want of a better term, 'person' (from the Latin *persona*) is the word most often used to translate hypostasis into English.

Applied to God, these terms were used to describe the Holy Trinity as three distinct hypostases in one divine nature (*physis*) or essence (*ousia*). Christ, on the other hand, is one hypostasis (the Second Person of the Trinity) in two natures: his divine nature and his human nature, which he has assumed through the Incarnation. A caveat to this description is that while such terms as 'being' are a helpful condescension to human limitations, in reality God is beyond any category, whether of being or any other. Here it must be noted that the comparison of human and divine hypostases can only be taken so far. The divine hypostases are not simply very large versions of human hypostases.

Theodore's statement that 'every image is the image of a hypostasis, and never of a nature' simply states that the connection of an image to its prototype is via its *likeness* to the unique hypostasis or person in whom these natures exist, and not by any identity of nature. This modality is essential for understanding how an image partakes of its original and what exactly it captures of it, and for grasping the dynamic aspects of personhood and imaging.

Iconodules never claimed that a panel of wood and paint shared the same nature as Christ, be it his divine nature or his human nature. An icon's nature is that of wood and paint and always remains so, but because of the connection between image and hypostasis, someone's view of Christ will be reflected in the way they treat his image.

The Orthodox Response to Iconoclasm

Theodore links hypostasis with the subject's name, since the name denotes the unique person:

> We say that Christ is one thing and His image is another thing by nature, although they have an identity in the use of the same name.
> (Theodore, *On the Holy Icons* 1.11; 1981: 31)

While a name is not the actual person named, it is the person by association. Likewise, an image of a person is not that actual person, but is that person by association.

While icons do not attempt to *depict* Christ's divine nature, they do indicate its reality. For example, the Septuagint translation of Jehovah, O ΩN ('The One Who Is'), is often found written on the Cross within Christ's halo, which is a clear declaration of his divinity. Symbolically, heavenly blue is used for his outer garment to suggest this divinity, and earthly red for his inner garment to suggest the human nature he assumed. These colours constitute visual pointers to his divine and human natures respectively, but without presuming to depict them as such.

Alongside his assertion of identity between image and subject through their shared name, John explained that, while an image does share likeness with its prototype, there are always differences between them:

> An image is therefore a likeness and pattern and impression of something, showing in itself what is depicted; however, the image is certainly not like the archetype, that is, what is depicted,

in every respect—for the image is one thing, and what it depicts is another—and certainly a difference is seen between them, since they are not identical.

(*On the Divine Images* 3.16; 2003: 95)

The more stylized manner of depiction seen in traditional icons (as outlined on pp. 58–70) can be explained in part as the attempt to maintain awareness of this difference between the image—the type—and the person represented—the prototype; an icon is never more, nor less, than an icon. From the point of view of the icon tradition, therefore, more 'realistic' or naturalistic depictions, such as seen from the time of the Italian Renaissance, can give only the illusion of being true to reality, but in fact such naturalistic paintings are attempting to be something they can never be.

ICONS AFFIRM THE INCARNATION

The basis of the icon of Christ is the Incarnation, and the iconodule theologians repeatedly returned to this theme. Icons of God are possible because, by Christ's birth, God became flesh and therefore became visible and depictable. To make icons is to affirm the reality of this enfleshment of God, while to deny icons' validity is to deny the incarnation's reality. John of Damascus wrote:

> Of old, God the incorporeal and formless was never depicted, but now that God has been seen

in the flesh and has associated with humankind, I depict what I have seen of God.

(*On the Divine Images* 1.16; 2003: 29)

ICONS AFFIRM THE UNION AND DISTINCTION OF CHRIST'S DIVINE AND HUMAN NATURES IN HIS SINGLE DIVINE PERSON

As discussed above, the iconoclasts incorrectly believed that an image is an attempt to represent the *nature* of the person depicted. From this misconception, they saw only two alternatives for iconodules, both heretical. For them, icons of Christ either separate the human nature of Christ from his divinity and thus depict his humanity alone (the Nestorian heresy, which 'divided the one Son and Word of God into two sons'), or else icons attempt to depict the one fused, divine-human nature of Christ, in which case the iconodules must be Eutychian Monophysites, who assert a single nature in Christ.

The iconodule writers showed that this argument was faulty at its inception, for icons do not at all depict the nature of the persons represented, but their hypostases, within which the natures inhere.

Additionally, there was an inherent contradiction in the iconoclasts' assertion, given in the Hiereia Council, that the only proper way to honour and acknowledge the 'unspeakable and knowable unique hypostatic union of the two natures of a person who is signified as absolutely one' was for it to be 'believed with the heart and confessed with the mouth' (Sahas 1986: 80–1) but not to depict it. On the one hand, this statement affirmed God's enfleshment in Christ while, on the other, it denied that this flesh could be depicted.

Theodore's reply to this charge by the iconoclasts (*On the Holy Icons* 1.3) was that Christ 'is one and the same in His hypostasis, with His two natures unconfused in their proper spheres' (Theodore 1981: 22). Theodore explained that God did not become 'a mere man' in Christ, nor did he 'assume a particular man' but rather 'assumed the whole human nature'. This said, Christ's whole human nature was seen by others 'in an individual manner', as one who is born and grows, who eats and drinks, who is called Jesus of Nazareth. This man, who walked the earth, yet whose single hypostasis is divine, is depictable because he is a man of visible flesh.

THE DISTINCTION BETWEEN VENERATION AND WORSHIP

The iconoclasts had a practical concern that people would worship icons as idols. In response, John of Damascus made it clear that the Scriptures clearly distinguish between the worship or adoration (*latreia*) which is due to God alone, and veneration, or the paying of honour (*proskynesis*) which is due to holy people, places, and objects through which God comes to mankind. Other terms used for veneration as distinct from worship are the Latin *veneratio*, and, in Greek, *timesis* (honour) and *douleia* (service). St John explains:

The Orthodox Response to Iconoclasm

> Veneration (bowing down) is a symbol of submission and honour. And we know different forms of this. The first is a form of worship (*latreia*), which we offer to God, alone worthy of veneration. Then there is the veneration offered, on account of God who is naturally venerated, to his friends and servants.
>
> (*On the Divine Images* 1.14; 2003: 27)

He then gives examples of such veneration found in the Scriptures, including Joshua and Daniel venerating angels, Israel venerating the tabernacle and the temple, and Jacob bowing to the ground before his brother Esau.

Any expression of honour made in front of an icon, such as making the sign of the Cross or kissing it, is not directed primarily towards the icon in and of itself, but to the person depicted upon it. In the words of Nicaea II, beginning with a quotation from Basil the Great's words from his *On the Holy Spirit*: '"The honour to the icon is conveyed to the prototype." Thus, he who venerates the icon venerates the hypostasis of the person depicted on it' (Sahas 1986: 179). While the emphasis is on the honour due to the image's subject, the image is also worthy of respect and honour since it helps mediate this relationship.

ICONS AFFIRM THE GOODNESS OF MATTER

Perceiving that a broader suspicion of matter underlay iconoclasm, John of Damascus took particular pains to affirm the capacity of matter to mediate divine life. In *On the Divine Images* 1.16 (2003: 29) he writes: 'the body of God has become God unchangeably through the hypostatic union ... Therefore I reverence the rest of matter and hold in respect that through which my salvation came, because it is filled with divine energy and grace.' After this passage, John proceeds to mention physical things through which salvation has come to mankind, such as the Cross and the hill of Calvary. He is not therefore speaking of sacraments as such, in which a special blessing transforms the thing into something it was not before (the bread becomes the body of Christ, for example) but of the grace-bearing potential of matter in general, in which it is filled with God's 'grace and power', especially sacred objects that represent a holy person or thing, such as an icon of the Mother of God or a figure of the Cross.

ICONS AND SACRAMENTS

While Theodore also affirms that icons bear grace to the faithful, he is at pains to differentiate them from the sacraments. It may be that Theodore was clarifying what John of Damascus meant in his assertion that matter can be Spirit-bearing. While icons do indeed bear grace, Theodore agrees, they do not actually become the subject, as the bread and wine do in reality become the body and blood of Christ. Because the iconoclasts mistakenly thought that a true icon had to be of the same nature as its prototype, they asserted that the only true icon was therefore the eucharistic body and blood of Christ. Theodore explains that while icons are an *image* of Christ, the Eucharist *is* Christ:

> we confess that the faithful receive the very body and blood of Christ, according to the voice of God Himself [i.e. the Lord's words of the institution: 'Take, eat, this is my body …'], why do you talk nonsense as if the sacraments of the truth were mere symbols?
> (Theodore, *On the Holy Icons* 1.10; 1981: 30)

The iconoclasts had failed to perceive the difference between sacrament, image, and type when they wrote:

> The icon of [Christ's] flesh, handed down by God, the divine bread along with the cup of his life-giving blood from his side, was filled with the Holy Spirit. This is, therefore, the icon that has been proven to be true icon of the incarnate dispensation of Christ our God.
> (Sahas 1986: 94)

Theodore asserted that the Eucharist is not a form or type but is the very body and blood of Christ. This is not, however, the case with the icon, which remains wood and paint and is not the Lord's body. The icon's connection with Christ is through its likeness to him, while the body and blood of Christ *are* him.

THE DEGREES OF MATTER'S PARTICIPATION IN GRACE

Having clarified that an icon is not a sacrament, Theodore goes on to explain in more detail what it means that matter can be grace-bearing, even God-bearing (*theophoros*), by describing how things and persons participate in grace according to their capacities. It must be noted here that this grace is not to be understood as some created gift but as God himself in his outgoing and uncreated life or 'energies' (the *energia* of hesychastic fourteenth-century Orthodox theology). By this uncreated grace he reveals himself to his people and sustains all creation while preserving his divine otherness—God as he is in himself. This eternally ineffable and unknowable 'God as he is in himself' is what later Greek patristics, particularly St Gregory Palamas (*c*. 1296–*c*. 1357), came to call God's essence or *ousia* (see Meyendorff 2010).

Theodore explains that a saint shares in grace through a personal (hypostatic) union with Christ, in a synergy of wills that leads to deification. Non-human entities—material things and 'beings without reason'—on the other hand, share in divine grace by association or 'relative participation', not person to person.

In the case of the painted icon, this relative participation derives from it being an image of humans who bear divine energy because of their personal union with Christ. There is thus a hierarchy of transmission:

> What place is there where divinity [i.e. divine energy] is not present, in beings with or without

The Orthodox Response to Iconoclasm

reason, with or without life? But it is present to a greater or lesser degree according to the capacity of the nature which receives it. Thus, if one says that divinity is in the icon, he would not be wrong, since it is also in the representation of the Cross and in the other sacred objects; but divinity is not present in them by the union of natures, for they are not deified flesh, but by a relative participation, because they share in the grace and the honour.

(Theodore, *On the Holy Icons* 1.12; 1981: 33)

THE ICON AS A BOOK FOR THE ILLITERATE

Although Byzantine apologists for the icon gave this much less emphasis, the pedagogical potential of images was much highlighted in the West. Pope Gregory the Great (540–604) defended icons primarily on the grounds of their pedagogic role for the illiterate, famously writing in a letter to Bishop Serenus of Marseille:

> For what writing provides for readers, this a picture provides for uneducated people looking at it, for in it the ignorant see what they should follow and the illiterate read the same from it. Thus a picture serves as a text, especially for pagans.
> (Gregory the Great, Letter to Serenus; 2004: 745)

This accent on the icon as a book for the illiterate was doubtless influenced by the lower literacy rate in Western Europe compared to Byzantium. Various factors had contributed to this: the collapse of central government in the West after the fall of Rome; the growing divide between the written Latin of ecclesial use and the gradual evolution of Romance languages spoken by the people; the fragmented and unstable environment meant that ability with the sword rather than the quill held greater utility. One might dare to venture that another factor in this stress on the didactic potential of images was the more utilitarian bent of the Latin mind.

Whatever the degree and reasons for any difference in emphasis between East and West, the image and the word require each other to reach their full potentials. For the literate person, a picture can enrich the information conveyed through the word, while for the illiterate, images can rouse curiosity and invite them to investigate further through questioning others. St Basil the Great hints at this synergy of word and image in a sermon on the martyr Balaam (PG 31.489A4–B4, and quoted by John of Damascus in *On the Divine Images* 1:34, and also in the Acts of Nicaea II):

> Rise up for me, O radiant painters of athletic achievements, and magnify the mutilated image of the general by your arts. The context in which he was crowned, described more dimly by me, you make radiant with the colours of your wisdom. Overwhelmed by you, I will refrain from describing the martyr's deeds of valour.
> (Basil, quoted in John's
> *On the Divine Images* 1:34; 2003: 43–4)

The Orthodox Response to Iconoclasm

ICONS AND TRADITION

Iconoclasts asserted that icons were a novelty and foreign to the traditional teaching of the Church, that 'with the pretext of Christianity, [the devil] reintroduced idolatry unnoticeably' (Sahas 1986: 62). In response, iconodules went to great lengths to collect passages from early Fathers that affirmed icons and their veneration. Among others, John of Damascus quoted from Dionysius the Areopagite (believed then to be the first-century convert of Paul), Basil the Great, Gregory of Nyssa, Severianus of Gabali, John Chrysostom, and Athanasius of Alexandria, and notably also Eusebius of Caesarea, who according to the iconoclasts was an iconophobe.

Tradition, however, is not merely the repetition of what earlier Church authorities have written. Vladimir Lossky has described tradition as the life of the Holy Spirit within the Church (see Lossky 1957: 188). Assertions, whether they be written, material, or spoken, therefore had to be tested by Church councils and other means to see whether they accorded with this experience of life in the Spirit within the Church. Checks and balances were used to help this process, including Scripture, councils, writings of acknowledged saints, reason, and past practices of the church.

ICONS OF SAINTS

The weight of theological justification for icons rested primarily upon images of Christ, but this does not explain icons of saints. Nicaea II gave a pastoral justification for such icons, namely that these images inspire people to emulate the saints' lives, so that 'the more these are kept in view through their iconographic representation, the more those who look at them are lifted up to remember and have an earnest desire for the prototypes' (Sahas 1986: 179).

On a more theological level, John of Damascus asserts that saints are to be honoured as living icons of Christ, as kings of the King of kings, and as God-bearers through their faith and holy lives:

> The saints should be honoured as friends of Christ, as children and heirs of God [...] And if the Creator and Lord of all is called 'King of kings and Lord of lords' [1 Tim 6:15] and 'God of gods' [Deut 10:17] the saints are necessarily gods and lords and kings [...] I mean gods and kings and lords not by nature, but because they have ruled over and mastered the passions and have kept inviolate the likeness of the divine image, in which they were created (for the king's image is also called king), and have been united with God by their free will, and have received Him as dwelling within them, and by participation in Him have become by grace what he is by nature.
>
> (John of Damascus, *On the Orthodox Faith*, 88; 2022: 258–9)

It follows that, if the saints can be honoured—since they have 'kept inviolate the likeness of the divine image' — then they, like Christ, and as visible corporeal beings, can have images made of them.

ICONS, THE CROSS, AND THE GOSPELS

Iconodule writers pointed out that the iconoclasts did in fact have icons, only they did not acknowledge them as icons, namely the Gospels and the form of the Cross. Iconoclasts had always accepted the tradition that the Gospels and the image of the Cross were worthy of veneration. In fact, they often erected images of the Cross in place of the figurative works that they destroyed, or which had been destroyed by disaster. Hagia Irene in Constantinople, for example, still sports a large mosaic Cross in the apse that was installed by iconoclasts during its restoration after an earthquake in the eighth century.

The Fourth Session of Nicaea II pointed out that images of the Cross are not the Cross itself but an icon of it; they are 'the figure of the precious and life-giving Cross' and not the actual Cross (*Seven Ecumenical Councils*, p. 536). Since the iconoclasts allowed images of the Cross, then it was only consistent for them also to allow images of Christ and the saints. The written Gospels, which iconoclasts also honoured, are likewise a form of icon for they are signs written in ink on a surface and are not themselves the actual spoken words of Christ. Nicaea II reasoned that icons are therefore rightly to be honoured as an image or representation of words and deeds:

Also [we declare] that one may render to [icons] the veneration and honour […] that is paid to the form of the precious and life-giving Cross, to the holy Gospels, and to the other dedicated items. Also [we declare] that one may honour these by bringing to them incense and light, as was the pious custom of the early [Christians]; for 'the honour to the icon is conveyed to the prototype'.

(Sahas 1986: 179)

— 4 —

Icons and Imageless Prayer

It might at first seem strange that the main defenders of icons against the iconoclasts were monastics, ascetics seeking 'imageless prayer'. Taken in isolation, many passages from saintly ascetic writers might seem to suggest an antipathy to images and the use of the five physical senses. For example, in his *On Guarding the Intellect*, St Isaiah the Solitary writes that 'the monk should shut all the gates of his soul, that is, the senses, so that he is not lured astray' (Isaiah 1979: 37).

However, a closer consideration of the ascetic texts, and the context of the macrocosmic vision presented by such Fathers as Maximus the Confessor (580–662), make it clear that it is attachment to material things that is being warned against, rather than material things themselves, which, after all, are created by God. Seen in this context, icons play an important role in all three of the classical stages of spiritual progress, namely: purification, illumination (called natural theology or *physike theologia* in Greek), and union or deification.

The sobriety and ascetic features of people in icons encourage the struggle against sin that is necessary for the first stage of purification.

The icon's luminosity and its hierarchical and abstracted arrangement of nature (mountains, trees, etc.) aid the perception of the Holy Spirit at work within the created world, which is the essence of the second phase of spiritual progress, natural theology. The basis of this natural theology is that God the Logos created each thing with a unique *logos*—'Let there be light'; 'Let the earth put forth vegetation' (Gen 1:3, 11)—and these *logoi* or words remain active within what they have created. God not only creates, but also 'sustains all things by his powerful word' (Heb 1:3). These *logoi* can also be described as the rational principles at work in beings through which they participate in divine grace.

This phase of natural theology therefore constitutes believers' capacity to perceive created things not just as isolated entities but as living words of God 'speaking' of his love for them. In this way the believer experiences all people and things as theophanies and not just objects. Indeed, the Greek term translated as 'word' used in Heb 1:3 above is *rhema*, which denotes the spoken and therefore living word.

It is this capacity to see and meet God through his created material gifts that leads to the ascetic's non-attachment to material things. In that sense, icons exist to become redundant once they have led the praying viewer to the prototype. This in large part explains the deliberate stylistic 'imperfections' of traditional iconography, a sort of aesthetic affirmation of its being a forerunner and not the messiah himself. Its 'an-iconocity' is as much part of the image's

Icons and Imageless Prayer

ontology as is its iconicity. Icons are both cataphatic in affirming their likeness to divine things, and apophatic in asserting that the deity ultimately surpasses any created likeness or category.

The aesthetics of icons embody this living *logos*. One could say that icons suggest the fire of God's presence within his material creation and not merely creation's physicality. This artistic form of icons affirms not only the physical likeness of the bush that Moses saw but also the divine fire that burnt within the bush without consuming it. This aesthetic embodiment of the living *rhema* corresponds with the *enargeia* of which Tsakiridou writes (see pp. 8–10).

However, there is a tension in that, on the one hand, an Orthodox icon does not claim to depict this fire in and of itself but rather the specific person or thing that is a theophany or 'showing forth' of that divine fire; on the other hand, an icon cannot do justice to the likeness of its subject if it does not in some way aesthetically indicate the presence of that grace which is integral to the subject's transfigured state. Images of Moses' burning bush would not be a likeness of that bush if they did not indicate the presence of that fire, in whatever artistic way it might be hinted at.

The third stage of mystical theology—theosis, deification, or union—is epitomized by icons of saints, which remind the faithful that deification such as the saints have received is mankind's highest calling, and not such things as material wealth or human praise. Haloes signify this indwelling of the Holy Spirit, but, as Pentcheva's studies have admirably shown (2010; 2017), the broader icon tradition has used light in many other more ontological ways as well, such as in the play of light within the church through well-placed windows, in reflection off polished lamps and metallic relief icons, and in the lighting and swinging of chandeliers at high points of festal services.

Another role of icons is to sanctify the imagination. Idolatry (from the Greek *eidololatreia*, meaning 'worship of the form') is worship of an image, object, or person as God. More broadly, idolatry can be to confuse a false image of truth with the truth, to confuse caricature with fact. This latter can hold true of imagined images as much as of material images. The imagination therefore needs to be calibrated to align with truth, just as belief needs to be calibrated through exposure to written and spoken orthodox doctrine. John of Damascus explains that:

> everywhere we use our senses to produce an image of the Incarnate God himself, and we sanctify the first of the senses (sight being the first of the senses), just as by words hearing is sanctified.
>
> (*On the Divine Images* 1.17; 2003: 31)

— 5 —

The Use of Icons

The icon is above all a liturgical object, but how specifically it is used needs to be clarified. For brevity, the following descriptions refer primarily to how Orthodox Christians use icons. Some of these practices, such as the lighting of candles before icons, are shared with Catholics and other 'iconodule' Christian traditions such as High Church Anglicans, while other practices, such as kissing icons, tend not to be.

ICONS WITHIN THE LITURGY

Orthodox faithful, on entering a church, typically cross themselves and bow three times by way of venerating the whole church as a single icon. The panel icon they will first encounter on entering, sitting on a stand called an *analogion*, is that of the feast or saint of the day, or perhaps of the church's dedication. They will typically cross themselves, bow, and kiss this icon (the fullest form of veneration being to cross and bow twice, venerate, then cross and bow a third time). They then proceed with candles to the icon screen and venerate the icon of Christ, and then of the Mother of God, and then any other icons they desire, lighting their candles. In Catholic and High Church Anglican traditions, the faithful will generally light candles but not kiss the icons.

ICONS AND RITUAL

Sacred images are used ritually in a multitude of ways; the medium is chosen according to the icon's intended use. Two examples are as follows. The book of the Gospels is considered an icon, and in Orthodox practice this typically has an image of the Crucifixion one side and the Resurrection on the other. These are usually engraved, embossed, or in enamel to withstand regular handling, for the Gospel book is displayed on an analogion for veneration on Sundays, and is carried in procession during the liturgy at what is termed the Small Entrance.

Some ritualistic uses for icons require a cloth medium rather than paint or metal. During Good Friday and Holy Saturday, an embroidered image of Christ lying in the tomb, called the *epitaphios* in Greek (literally, 'upon the tomb') and *plashchanitsa* in Slavonic, is carried in procession, laid for veneration on a flower-decorated table that symbolizes the tomb, and then later placed on the altar.

ICONS IN ARCHITECTURAL SPACE

Apart from the icon screen, which may have up to five tiers of icons in the Russian tradition, a fully decorated Orthodox church interior will be covered

The Use of Icons

in frescos or mosaics. Although there is considerable variety of themes, the placement of subjects is determined theologically as a means of expressing God's activity in the world. The most common arrangement for a centrally domed church is as follows: Christ Pantocrator (Almighty) in the dome, directing and sustaining all things; angels and prophets in the drum that supports the dome; the four Evangelists in the squinches (the bent corners that unite the drum to the cubic apse); events in Christ's life around the upper tiers and on barrel vaults; standing saints, often martyrs, in the lower tier, as ones defending the paradisal nave. In the apse, which symbolizes the womb and place of the Incarnation, is typically depicted the Mother of God. Below, on the semi-drum, is the Apostles' Communion and hierarchs celebrating the Eucharist. Images in the narthex (vestibule), which is the place of purification and preparation, often depict ascetics.

For the basilican church type, which is the most common design of Western churches and also the earliest Eastern churches, such as St Demetrius in Thessaloniki, the iconography centres on the apse and the triumphal arch surrounding the apse. Apses often have depictions of Christ flanked by the Virgin Mary and one or more saints associated with the church. Many early Roman churches, such as Santa Prassede (mosaics *c.* 820), also have depictions on the triumphal arch of the New Jerusalem and heavenly worship, as described in the book of Revelation (Rev 1:21–2).

THE DIDACTIC ROLE OF IMAGES

Panel icons of feasts are designed to go hand in hand with the theological hymns sung at their feasts. Word and image mutually interpret the sacred event. Illuminated manuscripts will not merely illustrate what is written but add an interpretative layer. The mid-ninth century Byzantine Chludov Psalter, for example, depicts the soldier piercing Christ's side on the Cross just above an image of an iconoclast scrubbing out an image of Christ (Moscow, State Historical Museum, manuscript D.129, folio 67r). This illumination is thereby saying that by defacing Christ's image, the iconoclast attacks Christ just as did the soldier at Christ's crucifixion.

ICONS IN THE HOME

A devout Orthodox family will have a dedicated place for prayer, with icons, a candle, hand censer, and prayer books. It is in effect a little church. This is called the *eikonostasis* in Greek, and the *krasnyi ugol* (beautiful corner) in Russian. This beautiful corner is depicted in some Russian paintings, such as in *The Sick Man* by Vasili Maximov (1881), and also in novels, such as in Dostoyevsky's *Crime and Punishment*, where Raskolnikov observes in the pawnbroker's apartment that 'in the corner an icon-lamp was burning before a small icon'. Often the main icons, such as that of Christ and the Virgin, are hung across a room's corner.

The Use of Icons

ICONS IN PUBLIC LIFE

In Orthodox and Catholic countries, icons are commonly found in public places to support mindfulness of God in all walks of life: in public transport and cars; in roadside shrines outside churches or at the site of a road accident; above city gates; and worn on the person. The traditional narrative is that the First Iconoclasm of Byzantium began when Emperor Leo III had the 'Icon of the Chalke' removed from above the Chalke Gate of the imperial palace. This was such a powerful symbolic act that it sparked riots (Mango 1977: 1–6).

THE ICON AS SENSUAL TYPOS OR IMPRINT

All the material liturgical arts are not merely a disposable means to an end, or an adjunct to the written or spoken word, but are themselves an integral part of the divine economy that embraces all the five senses through their capacity to embody a union of spirit and matter. While acknowledging that the historical incarnation of God in Christ is the apex of God's embodiment, Maximus the Confessor also asserted that:

> The Word of God, very God, wills that the mystery of his Incarnation be actualized always and in all things.
> (*Ambigua* 7.22, translation in Maximus 2014: I, 107)

Bissera Pentcheva has done much in the academic

world to bring the icon back into its proper context, the sensual and performative realm of liturgy, describing the icon as an extension of God's incarnation in matter and the corresponding capacity of matter to convey spirit through synaesthesis. Pentcheva's book, *The Sensual Icon: Space, Ritual, and the Senses in Byzantium* (2010), shows that the painted image has not always ruled as the primary form of icon; in the centuries following the overthrow of iconoclasm it was the relief icon that was most valued. Especially in its metallic and jewelled forms, the relief icon helped liturgical art embrace the 'is-ness' of the sacred work as itself an incarnational object that through its synaesthesis unites light and matter, spirit and materiality. She shows that this shift correlated with the iconophiles' conflation of the concept of *eikon*/image with *typos*/imprint:

> The *eikon* as *typos* caused a shift away from painting as the ideal medium for icons in ninth-century Constantinople. It freed Byzantine image-makers from striving for pictorial naturalism. By avoiding the imitation of form, disclaimed by both Iconoclasts and Iconophiles as 'the deceit of painting', Byzantine craftsmen severed the metal relief icon from the classical tradition of *zographia*.
>
> (Pentcheva 2010: 121)

— 6 —

Icon Form and Theology

DOES THEOLOGY IMPACT THE FORM OF ICONS?

For all the variety of their forms, there remains something so characteristic of icons that most people immediately recognize them as icons, rather than ordinary works of art. This raises the question of the relationship between the material form of Orthodox icons—their 'style'—and their theological and liturgical function.

The past century has seen much debate among art historians and iconologists about the nature of this relationship and the relative importance of factors that influence the form of icons (for a more extended summary, see Justiniano 2017). However, six major factors under debate can be summarized as follows: 1. the icon's liturgical function; 2. to what extent the form of icons endeavours to depict humans and the world transfigured by the Holy Spirit; 3. the particular vision and personality of the artist; 4. the cultural and theological milieu of the maker and the commissioners; 5. the influence of pre-Christian portraiture and religious imagery, particularly that of Late Antiquity; 6. the use of aesthetic techniques to evoke in the 'viewer' something of the subject's ethos, what Cornelia Tsakiridou calls the artwork's *enargeia* (see pp. 8–10).

Before discussing the forms or styles of icons and their possible roots, the historical background to the debate needs to be understood. During the centuries that the Greek Orthodox Church was under the Turkish yoke (1453–*c*. 1830), and the three centuries or so that Russia was under increasing secular Western influence from the time of Tsar Peter the Great (ruled 1682–1725), the style of icons began to be influenced by the more naturalistic trends that then dominated Western European art. As discussed on pp. 75–8, from around the late thirteenth century the emphasis of Western liturgical art had begun to shift towards greater naturalism, culminating in the Italian Renaissance. In the Baroque period that followed we encounter an emphasis on intense emotion that often slips into sensuality, as can be seen, for example, in the marble sculpture 'The Ecstasy of Saint Teresa' by Gian Lorenzo Bernini, made for the Cornaro Chapel of Santa Maria della Vittoria in Rome.

It was not until the early twentieth century that appreciation of the traditional 'Byzantine' and medieval Western iconography experienced a resurgence. Major early figures in this revival were Pavel Florensky (1882–1937) in Russia, followed later by Leonid Ouspensky (1902–87) in the West, and Fotis Kontoglou (1895–1965) in the Greek-speaking world. Florensky's most influential work in this respect was *Iconostasis*, composed in 1922 (for an English translation, see Florensky 1996), and also his various essays and published lectures, including 'Inverse Perspective', delivered in 1920. A selection of these essays in translation can be found in Florensky 2022. Leonid Ouspensky's most influential works are *The Meaning of Icons* (first published in 1952, latest edition 1997), co-authored with Vladimir Lossky, and *The Theology of the Icon* (1992). Kontoglou was an icon painter and author of many essays on iconography, a selection of which can be found translated and discussed by Constantine Cavarnos (1992).

Because these three writers were trying to re-establish the dignity of traditional iconography against what they considered more secularized Christian art, they perhaps overstated the difference between the icon tradition and other art forms. More recent writers have tried to introduce a more multivalent appreciation of what constitutes authentic iconography, both from the past and going forward into the future. Already discussed above (p. 9) is Marsingell's emphasis on the continued dialogue between Roman Late Antique portraiture and Christian iconography, and Cornelia Tsakiridou's stress on the importance of the icon's capacity as an artwork to embody aesthetically what it depicts through its *enargeia*. While distinguishing secular art and the religious icon, both writers thereby wish to avoid an artificial schism between them. In Tsakiridou's words (2019: 52): 'The image, qua image, aesthetically, partakes in the divine life of its subject and is thus neither a thing nor a person, neither a physical object nor an imaginal one, but the coinhering expression of all these modalities.' One could say that, while these authors acknowledge that the icon is more than just art, they equally assert that it is at least art, and as such utilizes aesthetic techniques.

George Kordis, a practising icon painter as well as an academic, explains in his book *The Icon as Communion* (2018) his own understanding of aesthetic techniques in the service of liturgy and ascesis. He suggests, for example, that an icon's form 'must not be simple but composite, consisting of smaller units, which come together and exist in harmonious unity within their common rhythm […] These units are distinguished by, and receive their unique existence or hypostasis through line, which, as we have already said, is the mode of existence of colour' (Kordis 2018: 7).

Irina Gorbunova-Lomax (2018) has labelled Florensky and those following his track as 'essentialist', since, she believes, they assert that icons attempt to depict the spiritual essence of the feast or person and not just their hypostasis through their observable likeness. 'Essentialist' is, however, an unsatisfactory label, since it confuses the aesthetic meaning of the word essence with the theological meaning of essence (the Greek *ousia*) as God's ineffable, unknowable, and therefore undepictable being as he is in himself. When 'essentialists' use the term essence in relation to artistic forms, they are referring to an icon's need to indicate something of its subject's character or spiritual state as part of its likeness to his or her hypostasis. This character in fact forms part of their likeness, alongside their physical features.

Integral to Bissera Pentcheva's study on the affirmation of the sensual character of liturgical art is her emphasis on how individual liturgical arts are designed to be performative, to be part of the active liturgy and to embrace all the senses. Her cross-disciplinary study *Hagia Sophia: Sound, Space, and Spirit in Byzantium* (2017) draws on digital acoustic models, video, examination of liturgical texts and melodic structures, and the church's architectural detailing to reveal the remarkable community of skills required to make the masterpiece which is the church of Hagia Sophia.

Other thinkers, such as Archimandrite Silouan Justiniano (2017) have sought a unitive assessment of these variant views. The following statements are therefore to be taken as an outline of some of the more commonly stated—though not universally held—correlations between style and function, adaptation and continuity.

ORIGINALITY AND TRADITION

It is a common misconception that the parameters set by the icon's theological and liturgical tradition restrict artistic creativity. The icon tradition's emphasis is not on novelty, but on making images that fulfil their chief aim of mediating between the faithful and the persons and events depicted in the images. An almost scientific precision is required to achieve this.

The parameters set by the icon's function do not, however, deny the need for artistic skill and courage. When healthy, the icon tradition responds to changing cultural and theological demands, without being subservient to them. For a survey of how festal icons developed over the centuries in response to these demands, see *Festal Icons*, by Aidan Hart (2022). The fact that an informed viewer can determine both the provenance and date of an icon from its style alone proves that variety does exist, and that the tradition allows artistic freedom to respond to shifting needs. Traditional icons are original in so far as they seek to illuminate the divine origin of things rather than to be novel for novelty's sake.

The source of the variety within the icon tradition is not, however, limited to how an individual liturgical artist responds. These artists are part of a culture which in turn is influenced by other cultures. This is the theme of Tsakiridou's work *Tradition and Transformation in Christian Art: The Transcultural Icon* (2019). She traces how the icon type of the King of Glory (Man of Sorrows) was transformed as it was adopted by the Latin West from its Byzantine prototype, and again after its migration through Catholic missionaries into Mexico and the rest of the Americas.

PERSPECTIVE SYSTEMS AND LITURGICAL SPACE

The first thing that many people notice about icons is their unusual perspective systems, of which there are at least six. One is so-called inverse perspec-

Icon Form and Theology

tive, in which lines converge in the space in front of the icon rather than at a point on the imaginary horizon within or behind the icon. This has been variously explained as a means of opening into the liturgical space in front of the icon, as distinct from an imaginary space within the image; and as a sign that the icon depicts the icon's subject (Christ or the saint) as the primary contemplator, and therefore depicts things viewed from their viewpoint rather than from the view of the person standing in front of the icon.

The overall flatness of icons works the other way: this deliberate imperfection of the image invites the viewer to pass through and beyond the image to meet the depicted saint in a personal relationship. The icon thereby transcends mere illustration, which assumes that the subject is absent, and instead seeks to introduce the viewer to the saints, being present through the Holy Spirit. It literally re-presents the subject. It thereby makes real the 'communion of the saints', as described in the Apostles' Creed. In this sense an icon is a mirror, which necessitates the actual presence of the person mirrored.

Other perspective systems used by icons include multi-view perspective (see below); hierarchical, in which more important people are made larger; isometric, in which parallel sides are kept parallel, neither converging nor diverging; vanishing-point perspective, sometimes but rarely used, and usually with a number of vanishing points and therefore a version of multi-view perspective.

NOETIC INITIATION

Fundamental to Orthodox ascetic practice is belief in the faculty of the *nous* as the spiritual eye of the heart, which, when purified and illuminated by the Holy Spirit, perceives ineffable things. The icon tradition cannot be understood apart from this. St Macarius of Egypt (c. 300–91) wrote the following:

> The soul which has been made worthy of fellowship with the Spirit of [Christ's] light, and which has been illumined by the beauty of His ineffable glory after having prepared itself for Him as a throne [*kathedra*] and dwelling place [*katoiketerion*], becomes all light and all face and all eye.
>
> (*Macarian Homilies* II.1.2, trans. Alexander Golitzin 2002)

The English translation of *The Philokalia* renders *nous* as 'intellect', which its glossary describes as 'the highest faculty of man through which—provided it is purified—he knows God or the inner essences or principles [*logoi*] of created things by means of direct apprehension or spiritual perception' (*Philokalia*, vol. 4: 432). Many elements of the icon's form aim to shift the viewer from a solely rationalistic view of reality—one which is mathematical and quantitative—towards such a noetic view, which is personalist and qualitative. The icon tradition equally eschews sentimentality by uniting its aesthetics with asceticism. It strives to indicate the struggle required to obtain the beauty of holiness. It aims not just to present beauty, but to make the viewer beautiful.

Pavel Florensky, in his groundbreaking lecture 'Reverse Perspective', explained the perspective systems employed by icons as expressive of a contemplative world view as opposed to a mechanistic one:

> For in the final analysis there are only two experiences of the world—a human experience in a large sense and a scientific, i.e., 'Kantian' experience, just as there are only two attitudes towards life—the internal and the external, and as there are two types of culture—one contemplative and creative, the other predatory and mechanical.
>
> (Florensky 2022: 218)

Apart from the inverse perspective system that Florensky was primarily concerned with in his lecture, another system that icons use to encourage such a noetic or contemplative vision is multi-view perspective, in which an object such as a building is depicted from multiple vantages at once, something impossible for a viewer limited in space. The object is thus depicted as it is known by God, who is not limited in space. The same perspective system is used temporally, in which a person is depicted more than once in the same image, as with Christ in the Nativity icon where he is shown both in the manger and being washed.

Sacred events are depicted not just as raw facts, but in a way that suggests the *logos* of the event, its spiritual purpose, its *why* as well as its *what*. The Transfiguration icon, for example, shows the three apostles reacting differently to the vision, each according to his age and disposition. Also, a cave is often shown under both Moses and Elijah, filled with gold. This indicates that whereas in Old Testament times these prophets had only partial visions of God—Moses seeing only 'the back parts of God' while hidden in the cleft of a rock, and Elijah hearing 'a still small voice' while at the mouth of a cave—at the Transfiguration they encounter God face to face as the incarnate and transfigured Lord.

SYMBOLISM

Liturgical icons are material objects that denote something spiritual. In this sense, they are symbolic in the literal meaning of the Greek word, formed from 'throw' (*balo*) 'together' (*syn*). Although the words are sometimes used interchangeably, a sign is to be distinguished from a symbol. A sign relates one object to another object, while a symbol relates to something at a higher level than itself.

Signs came to be a larger feature of Western iconography than in Byzantium, a trend encouraged by the former's emphasis on the didactic role of imagery, signs being a form of pedagogic illustration. The Eastern Church's preference for depicting actual persons rather than symbolic representations of them—particularly when it came to Christ—is reflected in canon 82 of the Quinisext Council, also called the Council in Trullo (691–2). This canon was not accepted by the Church of Rome, which continued, for example, to use the image of the lamb to denote Christ. To stress the reality of the Incarnation in the divine person of Christ, the canon discouraged symbolic images of Christ, such as a lamb, in favour of his depiction as a real man. It decreed that:

> the figure in human form of the Lamb who takes away the sin of the world, Christ our God, be henceforth exhibited in images, instead of the ancient lamb, so that all may understand by means of it the depths of the humiliation of the Word of God, and that we may recall to our memory his conversation in the flesh, his passion and salutary death, and his redemption which was wrought for the whole world.
> (*Seven Ecumenical Councils*, p. 401)

Because the Eastern icon tradition emphasizes encounter with real people and events rather than narrative, it tends to use signs and symbols less than does post-medieval Western art. Exceptions are found in post-sixteenth-century icons of Russia, when many icons proliferated narrative detail and symbolism. This entailed more figures, and therefore smaller figures and faces. This in turn compromised the earlier emphasis on face-to-face encounter with a holy subject that the medieval icons encouraged, whose figures or faces tended to fill most of the panel.

When symbolism is used in traditional icons, some of it is overt and some is imbedded in the composition's geometry. As for icons of saints, signs are sometimes used to identify key features of the saint's earthly life. A martyr, for example, is usually shown holding a cross and with some bright red in their raiment.

Festal icons will often include Old Testament types, which are material symbols of spiritual truths. The writer to the Hebrews refers to such types when he writes of Old Testament traditions:

> They offer worship in a sanctuary that is a sketch and shadow of the heavenly one; for Moses, when he was about to erect the tent, was warned, 'See that you make everything according to the pattern [Greek: *typon*] that was shown you on the mountain'.
>
> (Heb 8:5)

Annunciation icons, for example, might include a structure behind Mary that doubles as a throne and a temple with a parted curtain, both typological images referenced by the feast's hymns. An Orthodox hymn in the Matins of Annunciation multiplies such typological references:

> Hail, holy Mother of God; hail, living Bush. Hail, Lamp; hail, Throne; hail, Ladder and Gate. Hail, divine Chariot; hail, swift Cloud. Hail, Temple; hail, Vessel of gold […] Rejoice, swift cloud.
>
> (*Festal Menaion*, p. 459)

The symbolic content of the visual tradition is only fully revealed when linked to the tradition of the word, be it written, hymnographic, or homiletic. The typological significance of the throne and building behind Mary mentioned above would remain hidden to viewers without their exposure to the tradition of the word. Concomitantly, a purely word-based approach, by not employing the five senses, would fail to affirm the physicality of the human person. The Old Testament is as much an affirmation of divine revelation through material objects (the Tent of Meeting and its furnishings, for example) and visual representations (prophetical dreams and visions) as it is through word, such as the Ten Commandments and the words of the prophets.

LIGHT

Although icons do use light to model form—what is closer is shown lighter than what is distant—its primary use is to indicate the ways that grace or divine energies act on created things, this grace being symbolized by light.

The interpenetration of grace and matter helps explain the more abstracted style of traditional icons as compared to more naturalistic styles such as are found, for example, in works of the Italian Renaissance. While icons cannot depict these divine *energeia* directly, they can *indicate* their effect on creatures. Just as at Christ's Transfiguration his glory was transmitted to Peter, James, and John through the radiance of his material face and garments, so too does an icon indicate the presence of divine grace through painterly techniques. To *depict* a reality and to *indicate* its existence are not the same. In this respect, the icon tradition has its own forms of apophatic theology (saying what God is not) and kataphatic theology (saying what God is like) as does the written tradition. An image is both like and unlike its prototype; just as the statement that 'God is love' (1 John 4:8) affirms the quality of divine love as manifested in his energy, while simultaneously falling infinitely short of its reality.

Four stylistic uses of light by icons can be identified as indicating divine grace, each corresponding to a different degree of divine activity:

1. *The golden background.* This symbolizes the sustaining omnipresence of God, who upholds all things and people in existence, the latter regardless of their moral state. In the words of Paul: 'In him we live and move and have our being' (Acts 17:28). When gold is not used for backgrounds, some other light-reflective or energy-giving colour is used, such as white or vermilion. By contrast, in the case of wall paintings a blue background is often used. In this instance the background indicates not the outgoing radiance of grace but its mysterious and infinite depth. Aesthetically, the coolness of its hue also helps to quieten the souls of the worshippers and so aid inner prayer and attentiveness during the liturgy.

2. *Haloes* represent the Holy Spirit dwelling in and shining out from those who, through faith and virtuous life, have become especially clear vessels of grace. While the sustaining power of the Spirit is

given to all persons regardless of their moral state or beliefs, this deifying power of the Spirit, symbolized by the halo, is a hypostatic union that can be effected only through the synergy of the saint's free will with divine grace:

> If you love me, you will keep my commandments. And I will ask the Father, and he will give you another Advocate, to be with you for ever. This is the Spirit of truth, whom the world cannot receive, because it neither sees him nor knows him. You know him, because he abides with you, and he will be in you.
>
> (John 14:15–17)

Church Fathers have used the image of iron in fire to indicate the preservation of distinction in the midst of this deifying union. John of Damascus writes:

> For just as iron plunged in fire does not become fire by nature, but by union and burning and participation, so what is deified does not become God by nature, but by participation.
>
> (*On the Divine Images* 1:19; 2003: 33).

Icons likewise use the interaction of light and paint to suggest this same union without confusion of divine fire with created matter, and, ultimately, of the Holy Spirit's deification of humans.

St Irenaeus of Lyons (*c.* 140–*c.* 202) countered the Gnostic heresies of his time by stressing that this deification transfigures the whole psychosomatic person, flesh as well as soul:

> The complete man is a mixture and union, consisting of a soul which takes to itself the Spirit of the Father, to which is united the flesh which was fashioned in the image of God [...] men are spiritual not by the abolition of the flesh [...] there would then be the spirit of man, or the Spirit of God, not a spiritual man.
>
> (Irenaeus, *Adversus Haereses* 5.6.1; 1969: 71)

3. *Chromatic radiance and translucency*. Although icons do make a very limited use of shadow (such as on the neck of the famous mosaic of Christ found in the imperial gallery at Hagia Sophia, Constantinople), painted icons are characterized by light radiating from within and all around, which is why chiaroscuro (the strong contrast of light and shadow) is not found in icons. To achieve this luminosity, the paint is often applied thinly so that some of the incident light passes through the paint layer, then reflects off the white gesso ground that lies behind, to re-emerge from within the icon as transmitted light.

4. *Assist* (calligraphic gold lines applied to painted areas). These lines are usually applied to inanimate things, such as garments or furniture. It is a form of highlighting, but on a deeper level it affirms the capacity of inanimate matter to be grace-bearing, just as were Christ's garments at his Transfiguration, which the Gospels say 'became dazzling white' (Matt 17:2).

In the Italian Renaissance period painters such as Raphael (1483–1520) and Michaelangelo (1475–

Icon Form and Theology

1564) shifted emphasis away from light as a symbol of spirit towards light to model material form. This trend continued into the subsequent Baroque, when painters such as Caravaggio (1571–1610) used light to create emotionally dramatic effects. It was to this end that Caravaggio developed the chiaroscuro technique, created by a single directional and external light source. This emphasis on created external light reflecting off surfaces—be it from the sun or an artificial source like a candle—compromised the artistic capacity to suggest divine and transfiguring light coming from within and all around. Chiaroscuro was not a mere stylistic innovation, but a sign of a change from a theocentric worldview towards an anthropocentric and humanist worldview, a forgetfulness of the noetic faculty in favour of rationalism, something discussed below, pp. 60–2.

BRIGHT SADNESS AND SOBRIETY

Newcomers to icons often comment on the saints' sad countenances. A single Greek term, *charmolype* ('joyful sorrow'), describes this union of joy and sadness. Among other things, this countenance reflects the continued co-suffering or com-passion that the saints in heaven experience for those struggling on earth.

The union of opposites epitomized in *charmolype*, the absence of agitated movements, and the calmness of expression in icons, are rooted in the ascetical virtues of joyful sobriety, *hesychia*, dispassion, and compassion. Hesychius of Jerusalem wrote to

Theodulus: 'Sobriety is the way of every virtue and every commandment of God. It is also called silence of the heart, and is the same as guarding the mind, kept perfectly free of all fantasies' (Hesychius, text to Theodulus, para. 3; 1963: 280). Paul refers to this same union of sobriety and compassion in 1 Thess 5:8: 'Since we belong to the day, let us be sober, and put on the breastplate of faith and love, and for a helmet the hope of salvation.'

— 7 —

Iconography beyond Traditionally Orthodox Countries

The liturgical art of the Catholic Church, and those Protestant traditions that accept images, has clearly followed a different trajectory from that of the Orthodox Church. Art expresses the *zeitgeist* of its parent culture, which in the case of the Christian traditions is set by their respective theologies. Thanks to ease of travel, colour printing, and icon exhibitions, Western Christendom has been massively exposed to the icon over the past century or so, and thereby also to the spiritual vision and theology of the Orthodox Church that gave rise to these icons. This re-encounter of Eastern and Western Christianity after centuries of relative separation has generated much interest, and countless books and conferences. The fruits and challenges of this encounter are manifold and complex; hence the following overview can only be skeletal, but, it is hoped, still helpful in suggesting avenues for further exploration.

This book ends with a brief overview of the contemporary situation with regards to liturgical art and its historical roots; how the icon tradition has re-entered the consciousness of people beyond traditionally Orthodox countries; and the effect this has had on discourse about art and social issues of concern, such as ecology and the nature of the human person. To understand the present situation with regard to icons outside traditionally Orthodox countries, we must first give an overview of the iconoclasms in the West that have created the nature, and sometimes absence, of sacred imagery in its present churches and public places.

THE FRANKISH RESPONSE TO NICAEA II

While the Church of Rome fully supported the canons of Nicaea II, its emphasis remained the didactic role of images. This pedagogical role of images had particular relevance in the West, where the Latin used for all its rites was incomprehensible to the majority of worshippers after at least the ninth century, and before that, in areas speaking Germanic, Celtic, or other non-Latin languages. The Western Church seems to have remained suspicious of any emphasis on the veneration of images and, at least in the early centuries, did not seem to clearly and consistently distinguish between a valid veneration of images and the worship due to God alone. While Gregory the Great (c. 540–604) obviously opposed any worship of images, he seems not to have made efforts to distinguish idolatrous worship from valid veneration. In his letter to Bishop Serenus of Marseille, Gregory admonishes the bishop for destroying icons, and while praising him for banning their worship

Iconography beyond Traditionally Orthodox Countries

(*adorare* in Latin), he promotes the retention of images only on the basis of their instructive role:

> For the worship [*adorare*] of a picture is one thing but learning what should be worshipped [*adorandum*] through the story on a picture is something else ... And so you should not break what has been placed in churches not for adoration *but simply to instruct the minds of the ignorant*. [italics added]
>
> (Gregory, Letter to Serenus; 2004: 745)

It was perhaps this emphasis on the narrative role of images that encouraged the Roman Church to give artists greater stylistic licence than did the Orthodox Church, where theology and form were more connected.

The seeds of this divergence may be traceable as far back as 790, to the adverse reaction of Charlemagne and his court to the Second Council of Nicaea, expressed in the *Libri Carolini* (790) and the Council of Frankfurt (794). Nicaea II had stated that 'to icons should be given due salutation and honourable reverence (*proskynesis*), not indeed that true worship of faith (*latreia*) which pertains alone to the divine nature' (*Seven Ecumenical Councils*, p. 550). That is, icons should be venerated but not worshipped. However, while this distinction is clear in the Greek, the very poor Latin translation used by Charlemagne and his scholars failed to transmit this distinction. Charlemagne's council and his court (though not the pope) consequently rejected Nicaea II, thinking it was teaching people to worship icons. For a discussion of *Libri Carolini*, see Chazelle 1986 and Gero 1973.

Ironically, by limiting the role of icons to being mere reminders of events, the *Libri Carolini* delegated the style of imagery from theology to the artist's imagination. It limited the function of icons to 'remind[ing] one of things that have happened' and denied that they could convey deeper matters, asserting that 'such things as are understood by reason and expressed in words can be expressed not by painters but by writers and through verbal discourse' (Davis-Weyer 1986: 103).

Nicaea II delineated the role of the sacred artist's imagination more firmly. The Sixth Session asserted that 'the making of icons is not an invention of the painters but an accepted institution and tradition of the catholic Church […] only the art is of the painter, whereas the disposition is certainly of the holy Fathers who erected [churches]' (Sahas 1986: 84).

For Fransesco Stella (2022), the Carolingian assertion of artistic form's independence from liturgy and theology offered the basis of what would become, albeit much later, a purely secular art: 'So the Carolingian West, by freeing artistic expression from worship, desacralizes it and makes it potentially open to every possible scheme and interpretation. The "secularization" of the West bestows upon art a public and private freedom' (Stella 2022: 44). The seeds were thus planted for the later movement of Western Church art towards greater naturalism, which first appears with the works of Giotto di Bondone (*c.* 1267–1337) and grows into the Italian humanist Renaissance.

Iconography beyond Traditionally Orthodox Countries

THE THIRTEENTH TO SIXTEENTH CENTURIES AND THE REVIVAL OF ARTISTIC NATURALISM

Intellectually, the eleventh to the sixteenth centuries in Western Europe saw the emergence of scholasticism's dialectical reasoning as the preferred approach to the quest for truth, a trend promoted through the new universities. Though many churchmen were involved in trying to integrate this rationalism with faith, the most influential came to be the Dominican friar Thomas Aquinas (*c.* 1225–74). Scholasticism's attempt to define everything rationally, including theology, naturally led to greater naturalism in ecclesiastical art. This shift towards greater scientific naturalism is epitomized in the mathematically precise vanishing point perspective system developed by Filippo Brunelleschi (1377–1446).

This intellectual climate that favoured greater naturalism in the arts was reinforced by socio-economic trends and the resulting shift in patronage. From around the early fourteenth century, Western European political structures gradually moved from small fiefdoms with their rural peasantry towards a mercantile and banking class system that fostered city states, centred on new cities fuelled by trade and commerce. Although the great cathedral-building enterprises begun in the mid-twelfth century continued into the fourteenth, they were no longer the focus of artistic creation; the secular wealthy rather than bishops increasingly dominated commissioned art. A consequence of this shift in patronage is the rise of secular portraiture, what could be called the new iconography of the growing commercial and mercantile classes. Hans Belting describes this as 'the era of the private image' (see Belting 1994: 409–90).

Western liturgical art contributed to this trend towards greater naturalism by emphasizing the human element of sacred events. Beginning with Giorgio Vasari's book *The Lives of the Most Eminent Painters, Sculptors and Architects*, published in two editions, the later appearing in 1568, historians credit Giotto di Bondone with beginning this thrust towards greater naturalism, through works such as his frescoes in the Capella dell'Arena, Padua (c. 1305). Vasari considered mimetic art to be far superior to the more abstracted art of 'the Greeks', as he called Eastern Orthodox Christians. He wrote that Giotto 'became such an excellent imitator of Nature that he completely banished that crude Greek style and revived the modern and excellent art of painting, introducing good drawing from live natural models' (Vasari 1998: 85). Considering Byzantine art so inferior, he praises Giotto for liberating Italian painting from the stagnant ponds of this 'Greek' art:

> In this [Giotto] style we can see how the [Byzantine] outline completely eclosing the figures, those eyes with their lustreless staring, the feet standing on tiptoe, the pointed hands, the absence of shadows, and the other monstrosities of those Greeks have all been abandoned, giving

place to genuine gracefulness in the heads and softness in the colouring.
(Vasari, *Lives of the Artists*, 1998: 171)

This trend, begun by Giotto, accelerated through to the Quattrocento Italian Renaissance, centred in Florence and Rome, and then on into the High Renaissance of the following century.

Giotto is often considered the founder of Renaissance painting. He wanted not merely to tell stories about past events but to paint his works so realistically that viewers felt they were present at these events. While Eastern Christian iconography sought to invite such participation through techniques of artistic abstraction that stimulated spiritual vision (the noetic faculty discussed on pp. 60–2), Giotto sought to do this by imitation, and therefore employed naturalism.

Recent art historians who, somewhat like Vasari, have not understood the noetic aim of Byzantine art have often labelled its iconography stilted and restrictive of artistic merit, while praising the new naturalism as liberating and more realistic. E. H. Gombrich, for example, writes of Byzantine art's 'rigidity', its 'frozen solemnity', and the 'spell of Byzantine conservativism' (Gombrich 1995: 201). By contrast, the icon traditionalist would consider naturalism such as Giotto's too constrictive, observing that it limits art to what is perceptible to the visual and rational faculties while neglecting what the noetic faculty sees (see for example, Sherrard 1990: 85–107). An iconographer would say that naturalism is in fact less realistic, for its avoidance of abstraction limits what it can indicate of spiritual realities.

THE REFORMATION AND ICONOCLASM

Although Martin Luther himself was not opposed to images, the early Reformers Thomas Müntzer and Andreas Karlstadt initiated the first iconoclasm in Wittenburg in the 1520s. Luther's primary focus was on idolatry in the deeper sense, such as justification by works (see Stjerna 2015: 52). He in fact opposed iconoclastic activity being presented as a 'good work' by the iconoclasts, and linked it to insurrection and civil disorder (Brecht 1990: 137–194). Luther wrote:

> I am not of the opinion that all arts are to be cast down and destroyed on account of the gospel, as some fanatics protest; on the other hand, I would gladly see all arts, especially music, in the service of Him who has given and created them.
> (Luther, Preface to *Spiritual Hymn Booklet*; 1997: 196–7)

This pragmatic position clashed with that of the more radical reformers. In the words of Leslie P. Spelman: 'Luther was inclined to allow anything not condemned by the Bible, while Calvin went so far as to allow nothing which was not expressly approved by the Bible' (Spelman 1951: 166).

The reforming theology of its leading proponents, such as Karlstadt, Huldrych Zwingli, and John Calvin, opposed images on the basis that they contravened the First and Second Commandments. As can be seen from his *Institutes of Christian Religion*, Calvin saw no place for painting or sculpture within the church and spoke against the use of religious images as educational aids for the illiterate (Calvin 1845: 99). He insisted that only visible things found in nature could be depicted, and extended the prohibition of depicting the invisible Godhead, found in Nicaea II, to depictions of Christ. In *Institutes* 1.11, Calvin tried to substantiate his view that 'Scripture declares images to be teachers of vanity and lies' (1.11.5, in Calvin 1845: 95) with appeals to the early Church, erroneously asserting in 1.11.13 that for 'five hundred years, during which religion was in a more prosperous condition, and a purer doctrine flourished, Christian churches were completely free from visible representations' (Calvin 1845: 105). The abundance of extant works from that period show this statement to be blatantly false.

Calvin also called upon some Church Fathers in support, including those from the East, with whose writings he had only passing familiarity, and that primarily via Latin sources (Lane 1991: 48). His enthusiastic refutation of Nicaea II in the *Institutes* seems to be based solely on his encounter with that Council via its faulty translation used in *Libri Carolini* (Payton 1997: 472). In 1.11:11 Calvin includes a complete dismissal of any differentiation in meaning between veneration and worship, or between a correctly understood sacred image and an idol that usurps God's place in people's worship (Calvin 1845: 104).

Aside from the theological arguments, another significant factor in the Reformers' hostile stance towards images was their strong desire to distinguish themselves wholesale from Roman Catholicism and the abuses with which it had become associated, such as the sale of indulgences and simony.

Subsequent to this movement, iconoclasm soon became the norm in the newly Reformed territories and cities, which were mostly in northern Europe. The transition was sometimes violent, with destruction of images often prompting riots, as in Basel (1529), Geneva (1535), and Scotland (1559), while at other times it was a more gradual and orderly process, organized by the authorities (see Wallace 2014).

In Britain the iconoclasm was activated in various ways and by various people. Under the influence of Thomas Cranmer, King Edward VI in 1550 issued religious reforms in an Act of Parliament 'for the abolition and putting away of divers books and images' (Heal 2005: 263–4). Further destruction and whitewashing of images followed during the Civil Wars (1642–51), executed mainly by Parliamentarian armies (see Spraggon 2003). While scholars disagree whether the Puritan leader of the Parliamentarian army, Oliver Cromwell (1599–1658), actively supported this iconoclasm and gave orders to his troops to that end, it is clear that he knew his troops were destroying images wholesale and did nothing or little to prevent them. They were, in any event, acting according to ordinances enacted by Parliament. The May 1644 Ordinance for the Further Demolishing of Monuments of Superstition and Idolatry explicitly directed 'That all Representations of any of the Persons of the Trinity, or of any Angel or Saint, in or about any Cathedral, Collegiate or Parish Church, or Chappel, or in any open place within this Kingdome, shall be taken away, defaced, and utterly demolished' (Firth and Rait 1911).

ICONOGRAPHY AND THE SCIENTIFIC REVOLUTION OF THE SIXTEENTH TO EIGHTEENTH CENTURIES

A culture's art is an image of that culture's dominant world view. Such thinkers as Philip Sherrard in his *Human Image: World Image* (1992) and Edwin Burtt in *The Metaphysical Foundations of Modern Science* (2003) have shown that the scientific revolution accomplished between the sixteenth and eighteenth centuries constituted a shift from a sacred view of the world and of mankind's place in it to a mechanistic one in which mathematics and rationalism effectively became the new religion.

An early proponent, and then figurehead, of this new world view is generally considered to be the mathematician and philosopher René Descartes (1596–1650), for whom is named the Cartesian philosophical method, espoused in his work published in 1637, *A Discourse on the Method of Correctly Conducting One's Reason and Seeking Truth in the Sciences*. This new mathematical-philosophical system effectively made God the divine clockmaker who created the world as a self-sufficient entity and then departed, having provided man with his rational faculties to study it as a sort of complex mathematical machine. Eventually, God was omitted from the equation to leave the purely materialistic and mechanistic atheistic world view that dominates contemporary science.

This supremacy of scientific rationalism naturally had a profound effect on the artistic movements and liturgical art of those three centuries, such as the replacement of the 'dimension' of the sacred with the mathematical dimension of depth in physical space. The chief artistic movements over these three centuries are the Baroque, Rococo, Romanticism, Realism, and the Neoclassical. Whether they are proponents of this new rationalism or reactions to it, they nevertheless use the same language. The old use and understanding of icons continued in the Christian East, which saw rationality as only one of the human faculties to be used for understanding and life.

The end of the eighteenth century began to see the inevitable rejection of both this mathematical and quantitative approach, and the sentimental view of the world epitomized in much of the official Salon art of the Academies. To this modernism we now turn.

— 8 —

The Return of the Icon to Western Europe

The inevitable reaction to the stilted conservatism of the Academies came under the broad name of Romanticism, a movement characterized by the freedom of the individual over structures, and of intense emotion rather than rationalism—especially from an experience of the sublime. This movement had two consequences in relation to art and iconography.

THE ROMANTIC MOVEMENT AND THE ICON REVIVAL IN THE WEST

On the one hand, the Romantic world view introduced a much greater emphasis on the individual artist's personal vision over tradition, which in turn led to a proliferation of artistic movements. Where refinement and order had been the qualities previously sought, now novelty and revolution became the new virtues. Robert Hughes traces this 'counter-revolution' in his *Shock of the New: Art and the Century of Change* (1991). This trend within secular art has naturally imposed its challenges and influences on liturgical art.

On the other hand, Romanticism's rejection of a rationalistic world view began to open art historians' minds to the virtues of medieval icons and the world view behind their forms and uses. The painter and art critic Roger Fry (1866–1934) was particularly influential in asserting the value of Byzantine art. In particular, he often defended many of the emerging modern art movements as expressing similar values to that of Byzantine icons. He wrote in a letter to the editor of *The Burlington Magazine* (March 1908) about Cézanne and Gauguin, their works then being on display at the International Society in London: 'They are not really Impressionists at all, they are proto-Byzantines rather than Neo-Impressionists. They have already attained to the contour, and assert its value with keen emphasis' (Fry 1908: 374).

This renewed appreciation of traditional iconography gained impetus, or even began, with the Slavophile movement in Russia. In reaction to the extreme Westernizing policies implemented from the time of Peter the Great, from about 1830 onwards anthropologists, art historians, and authors began to explore the merits of medieval Russian art and thought. Among its key figures were Aleksey Khomyakov (1804–60), Ivan Kireyesvsky (1806–56), and, later, Pavel Florensky (1882–1937).

Among other things, in the opening decades of the twentieth century, this Slavophile movement led to the cleaning of medieval icon masterpieces to reveal their original brilliance. What became the most famous icon thus revealed beneath numerous overpaintings was the Trinity icon by Andrei Rubliev (painted c. 1425). Its first cleaning was undertaken in 1904, and a more professional restoration was undertaken in 1918–19 (see Bunge 2007). Though the atheistic Soviet regime destroyed countless icons, mosaics, and frescoes, it did agree to preserve some, including the Trinity icon, as being national treasures. Many privately owned portable icons were also saved by refugees fleeing to the West.

In the wake of this revival, icons began to be collected, exhibited, and studied in Western Europe. The writings and icons of Leonid Ouspensky and Fotis Kontoglou (mentioned on p. 55) were key to this revival. In the scholarly world, studies on Late Antiquities and Byzantine art flourished. Leading early figures include Viktor Lazarev (1995; 2001 for a collection of his papers); Ernst Kitzinger (2002; 2003); Otto Demus (1998); and Kurt Weitzmann (1973; 1976).

THE SECOND VATICAN COUNCIL (1962–1965)

Though the Second Vatican Council (Vatican II) promoted art in the Catholic Church, the actual result was a considerable reduction in images and a tendency towards the white-walled minimalism that was the architectural trend of the time. Pope John XXIII defined the purpose of Vatican II as the 'modernization of the Church after twenty centuries of life'. One of its liturgical aims was to encourage 'moderation' in the number of sacred images and their correct use, and to give greater stylistic freedom to makers of sacred art, as long as their works were duly reverend and honourable. The *Sacrosanctum Concilium* VII states the following:

> The art of our own days, coming from every race and region, shall also be given free scope in the Church, provided that it adorns the sacred buildings and holy rites with due reverence and honour. … The practice of placing sacred images in churches so that they may be venerated by the faithful is to be maintained. Nevertheless, their number should be moderate and their relative positions should reflect right order. For otherwise they may create confusion among the Christian people and foster devotion of doubtful orthodoxy.
> (Second Vatican Council 1963, para. 123 and 125)

Judging by the increasing number over the past few decades of Catholic iconographers and of icons being commissioned for Catholic churches, there appears to be a reversal of this minimalism and a movement back towards more traditional figurative art.

THE ICON'S INFLUENCE ON EARLY-TWENTIETH-CENTURY ART

An increasing body of literature is revealing the influence that the icon tradition had on the abstract art movements of the early twentieth century. This is not surprising, given that most of its founders came from traditionally Orthodox countries. The founder of modern abstract sculpture, Constantin Brancusi, was from Romania. Once, when his friend Petre Pandrea was praising his sculpture, Brancusi retorted that all he had done was to set up a Paris branch of his homeland's Tismana Orthodox Monastery (for little-known elements of Brancusi's life and beliefs, see Brezianu and Geist 1965). Wassily Kandinsky, the founder of modern abstract painting, and author of *The Spiritual in Art*, was from Russia. Matisse was not influenced by icons as such, but he did say that medieval Russian icons confirmed the correctness of his direction: referring to Russian icons, he stated that 'you surrender yourself that much better when you see your efforts confirmed by such an ancient tradition. It helps you jump over the ditch' (Ham 1995: 178). For an assessment of the spiritual roots of these and other abstract artists, see John Golding's *Paths to the Absolute* (2000).

Numerous elements of early Modernism were influenced by the icon tradition, but perhaps chief among them were: 1. truth to the flatness of the picture plane; 2. the use of abstraction to indicate invisible realities; 3. the use of flat areas of colour rather than shadow to model form.

Although abstraction now tends to be understood as a movement away from realism, for the early abstractionists it was the opposite. Their abstractionism was an attempt to manifest reality, to indicate the energetic essence of things, what Church Fathers like Maximus the Confessor called their divine *logoi*. Maximus wrote:

> If, instead of stopping short at the outward appearance which visible things present to the senses, you seek with your intellect to contemplate their inner essences [*logoi*], seeing them as images of spiritual realities, or as the inward principles of sensible objects, you will be taught that nothing belonging to the visible world is unclean.
>
> (Maximus, *Various Texts*, First Century, par. 92, in *Philokalia*, vol. 2: 185)

This search was fundamental for Brancusi, who said that 'the artist should know how to dig out the being that is within matter and be the tool that brings out its cosmic essence into an actual visible essence' (Bach, Rowell, and Temkin 1995: 23).

The flow can run the other way as well, where a seeker passes through such abstractionism as part of their spiritual quest, eventually to arrive at conversion, and back to the iconography that partly inspired that abstract art. An example of such a path is that of St Sophrony Sakharov (1898–1993), as outlined in Sister Gabriella's book, *Seeking Perfection in the World of Art: The Artistic Path of Father Sophrony* (2019).

Some commentators, such as Robert Nelson (2007), argue that beneath the veneer of secularism all art in fact remains spiritual, albeit not necessarily aligned with a religious tradition, and that the mysteries of religious practice are abstracted and continued through all stages of secularism in European culture.

THE ICON TODAY

The increased awareness of the icon tradition over the past century, and in countries not traditionally Orthodox, has had several consequences. First, there has been a marked increase in the number of icons commissioned by non-Orthodox churches. In Britain, most Anglican cathedrals have at least one panel icon; Westminster Abbey has three, and many parish churches also display icons. Catholic churches are likewise experiencing a revival of their use.

A second outcome is the proliferation of icon-painting courses in the West, some just five-day workshops, others more extensive, such as the Certificate in Icon Painting run by the King's Foundation School of Traditional Art, London, and the recently founded St Tikhon's Art Institute, Waymart, Pennsylvania.

Another effect has been a marked growth in interest within the academic world and among museums. Not only have major museums such as the Metropolitan Museum of Art in New York put on large exhibitions (Africa and Byzantium, November 2023–March 2024), but also smaller galleries, such as the Auckland Art Gallery (Heavenly Beings: Icons of the Christian Orthodox World, April–September 2022).

Within the icon-painting community, the revival has led to a lively debate about what constitutes traditional iconography, some of the issues having been covered in this book. The consensus is that the tradition is a living one, which not only responds to changing pastoral and doctrinal needs, but also affirms, adapts, and sometimes adopts elements of the particular culture for which the iconography is being made. In his book *Metamorphosis: The Transfiguration in Byzantine Theology and Iconography* (2005), Andreas Andropoulos illustrates this capacity of icons to adapt to changing theological emphases by tracing the history of Transfiguration depictions, relating them to the philosophical, social, and ecclesial changes that inspired these iterations on the theme.

In more recent times, stylistic changes within the tradition can be seen in various quarters. The Neo-Coptic style, initiated by Dr Isaac Fanous (1919–2007), for example, fuses elements of medieval Coptic iconography with Cubism. Father Gregory Krug (1908–69) managed to integrate into his icons some elements of the modern art movements that were part of the Parisian milieu in which he lived. Archimandrite Zenon (Teodor) from Russia is doing much to open Russian icon painting to influences from early Byzantine and Western Roman influences, such as mosaics from Ravenna. Ivan Polverari, a Catholic iconographer in Italy, has developed a rhythmic style that is both unique and traditional. The author often draws on Romanesque and Anglo Saxon sources for inspiration where appropriate for his commissions.

The icon tradition is not however limited to the liturgical object in itself but extends to its use. Although many panel icons are appearing in Catholic and Anglican churches and beyond, the question arises whether they are being used to their full potential: although their pedagogical value is widely acknowledged, are they being venerated and actively used in liturgical ritual? In her book *Icons in the Western Church*, Jeana Visel, writing as a Roman Catholic, has called for sacred imagery to be much better integrated into Catholic liturgy than it currently is. David Clayton has done much to integrate iconography into the Catholic milieu through his writings, such as *The Way of Beauty: Liturgy, Education, and Inspiration for Family, School, and College* (2015).

Since icons have become so popular, the number of unskilfully made icons in churches has increased. This raises the issue of the extent to which the artistic quality of an icon affects its spiritual effectiveness. Here it might be noted that an icon has two roles: one is for veneration, in which case the quality of the image is of secondary importance in that it is the subject being venerated and not the icon itself. A second role of icons is, however, compromised by lack of skill, namely the potential of their form to help transform the way the faithful see the world (as discussed on pp. 53–70). Fr Maximos Constas discusses this transformative power of icons through their form as well as through their subject in his work *The Art of Seeing: Paradox and Perception in Orthodox Iconography* (2014).

ICONS AS A PARADIGM TO ADDRESS CONTEMPORARY ISSUES

In recent decades, theologians, philosophers, and thinkers have used the icon's theology to seek responses to contemporary issues such as ecology, science and religion, the role of art, and the nature of the human person. Philip Sherrard in his *Rape of Man and Nature* (2015) and John Chryssavgis and Bruce Foltz in *Toward an Ecology of Transfiguration: Orthodox Christian Perspectives on Environment, Nature, and Creation* (2004), for example, have traced the cause of the ecological crisis back to a faulty worldview in which secular man ceases to view creation as an icon of its Creator's glory and wisdom.

The ecological crisis in the world has also had an effect in the opposite direction, challenging the icon tradition to respond. Henry Maguire has shown in his book *Nectar and Illusion: Nature in Byzantine Art and Literature* (2021) that nature figured much more in Byzantine church decoration before iconoclasm. Though perhaps not openly calling for a greater re-incorporation of nature into contemporary iconography, this might be suggested in some of his observations. For example, in Chapter 4, 'Nature and Abstraction', Maguire contends that pre-iconoclastic churches represented nature in all its specificity, whereas after iconoclasm, 'motifs from nature were represented in an undefined manner that clearly demonstrated their inferior status' (Maguire 2021: 106).

In their historical study, *The Penultimate Curiosity*, the artist Roger Wagner and scientist Andrew Biggs (2016) challenge the misconception that scientific study must inexorably conclude in atheism, showing on the contrary that many of the greatest scientists were motivated by the desire to explore

God's creation as a manifestation and image of divine wisdom. Although their hypothesis does not draw directly on the icon tradition, it parallels it. The authors fittingly conclude their study with the words inscribed above the entrance to the Cavendish laboratory: 'The works of the Lord are great, sought out of all them that have pleasure therein' (Ps 111:2, Coverdale translation).

The English theologian Andrew Louth contests the equation of originality with novelty in much contemporary art, contrasting this with the role of art to image pre-existing realities and to mediate between higher and lower realms:

> Images mediate; images bring one thing in relation to another; images make possible meaning [...] When the artist makes an image or icon, he is contributing to the symphonic unity of the world or cosmos in all its senses.
>
> (Louth 1996: 166)

Pavel Evdokimov explores the charisms of beauty and culture in general through the lens of iconology in *The Art of the Icon: A Theology of Beauty* (1972).

The nature of the human person is explored in Paulos Gregorios's work *The Human Presence* (1980). Gregorios challenges the very concept and naming of 'nature' as some entity distinct from the human person, saying that this separation of mankind and the rest of the cosmos has roots in neither the Hebrew nor Christian tradition. Following St Gregory of Nyssa, he asserts that the human person's destiny, as a union of body and spirit, is to be a mediator, prophet, priest, and royal artist:

> Since through his body and soul man becomes a participant in both the intelligible and the sensible, he is the citizen of two worlds, yet a whole being, with a special vocation to spread the grace of God through the whole of creation, animate and inanimate.
>
> (Gregorios 1980: 65)

As a physical work of art, made to participate in sacred ritual, to mediate between heavenly and earthly realities, and underpinned by a profound theology, the icon promises to continue providing rich seams for those searching for a holistic and incarnational world view.

Bibliography

Alexander, Paul J. 1958. *The Patriarch Nicephorus of Constantinople: Ecclesiastical Policy and Image Worship in the Byzantine Empire.* Oxford: Clarendon Press.

Andropoulos, Andreas. 2005. *Metamorphosis: The Transfiguration in Byzantine Theology and Iconography.* New York: St Vladimir's Seminary Press.

Athanasius of Alexandria. 2011. *On the Incarnation of the Word*, trans. John Behr. Popular Patristics Series 44. New York: St Vladimir's Seminary Press.

Bach, Friedrich, Margit Rowell, and Ann Temkin. 1995. *Constantin Brancusi.* Philadelphia: Philadelphia Museum of Art.

Belting, Hans. 1994. *Likeness and Presence: A History of the Image before the Era of Art*, trans. Edmund Jephcott. Chicago: University of Chicago Press.

Bigham, Steven. 2004. *Early Christian Attitudes toward Images.* New Hampshire: Cocheco Falls Publishing. https://www.smashwords.com/books/view/609356

—2008. *Epiphanius of Salamis: Doctor of Iconoclasm? Deconstruction of a Myth.* Patristic Theological Library 3. New Hampshire: Orthodox Research Institute.

—2015. 'Romanesque Art and Icons', in *Romanesque Art and Icons and Other Iconographic Studies.* Smashwords Platform: https://www.smashwords.com/books/view/598136

—2017. *Cinq documents originaux pour accompagner le livre Épiphane de Salamine, docteur de l'iconoclasme?* Smashwords Platform: https://www.smashwords.com/books/view/707302.

Boeckl, Christine. 2019. 'The Legend of St. Luke the Painter: Eastern and Western Iconography', in *Wiener Jahrbuch für Kunstgeschichte* 54/1. https://doi.org/10.7767/wjk.2005.54.1.7

Brecht, Martin. 1990. *Prophets, Enthusiasts, Iconoclasts, Fanatics, and the Peasants' War*, ed. James L. Schaaf. Minneapolis: Fortress Press.

Brezianu, Barbu, and Sidney Geist. 1965. 'The Beginnings of Brancusi', in *Art Journal* 25/1: 15–25.

Bunge, Gabriel. 2007. *The Rublev Trinity.* New York: St Vladimir's Seminary Press.

Burtt, Edwin A. 2003. *The Metaphysical Foundations of Modern Science.* New York: Dover Publications.

Calvin, John. 1845. *Institutes of the Christian Religion*, trans. Henry Beveridge. https://ccel.org/ccel/calvin/institutes

Cavarnos, Constantine. 1992. *Byzantine Sacred Art: Selected Writings of the Contemporary Greek Icon Painter Fotis Kontoglou on the Sacred Arts according to the Tradition of Eastern Orthodox*. Boston: Institute for Byzantine & Modern Greek Studies.

Chazelle, Celia. 1986. 'Matter, Spirit, and Image in the Libri Carolini', in *Recherches augustiniennes* 21: 163–84.

Chryssavgis, John, and Bruce V. Foltz (ed.). 2013 [2004]. *Toward an Ecology of Transfiguration: Orthodox Christian Perspectives on Environment, Nature, and Creation*. Fordham: Fordham University Press.

Clayton, David. 2015. *The Way of Beauty: Liturgy, Education, and Inspiration for Family, School, and College*. New York: Angelico Press.

Clement of Alexandria. 1885. *The Paedagogus*, vol. 3, trans. William Wilson. Ante-Nicene Fathers 2. https://www.newadvent.org/fathers/02093.htm

Constas, Maximos. 2014. *The Art of Seeing: Paradox and Perception in Orthodox Iconography*. Alhambra, CA: Sebastian Press.

Davis-Weyer, Caecilia (ed.). 1986. *Early Medieval Art 300–1150*. Toronto: University of Toronto Press.

Demus, Otto. 1998. *Studies in Byzantium, Venice and the West*. London: Pindar Press.

Descartes, René. 2008 [1637]. *A Discourse on the Method of Correctly Conducting One's Reason and Seeking Truth in the Sciences*, trans. Ian Maclean. Oxford: Oxford University Press.

Eire, Carlos M. N. 1986. *War against the Idols: The Reformation of Worship from Erasmus to Calvin*. Cambridge: Cambridge University Press.

Eusebius. 1965. *The History of the Church*, trans. G. A. Williamson. Harmondsworth: Penguin.

Evdokimov, Pavel. 1989 [1972]. *The Art of the Icon: A Theology of Beauty*. Redondo Beach, CA: Oakwood Publications.

The Festal Menaion, trans. Mother Mary and Kallistos Ware, 1969. London: Faber & Faber.

Finney, Paul Corby. 1994. *The Invisible God: The Earliest Christians on Art*. Oxford: Oxford University Press.

Firth, C. H., and R. S. Rait (ed.). 1911. 'May 1644: An Ordinance for the further demolishing of Monuments of Idolatry and Superstition', in *Acts and Ordinances of the Interregnum, 1642–1660*. London: His Majesty's Stationery Office.

Florensky, Pavel. 1996. *Iconostasis*, trans. Donald Sheenan and Olga Adrejev. New York: St Vladimir's Seminary Press,

Bibliography

—2022. *Beyond Vision: Essays on the Perception of Art*, ed. Nicoletta Misler, trans. Wendy Salmond. London: Reaktion Books.
Fry, Roger. 1908. Letter to the *Burlington Magazine*, March 1908, quoted in Christopher Reed, *A Roger Fry Reader*, p. 73. 1996. Chicago: University of Chicago Press.
Gabriella, Sister. 2019. *Seeking Perfection in the World of Art: The Artistic Path of Father Sophrony*. Tolleshunt Knights: Stavropegic Monastery of St John the Baptist.
Gero, Stephen. 1973. 'The Libri Carolini and the Image Controversy', *Greek Orthodox Theological Review* 18: 7–34.
Golding, John. 2000. *Paths to the Absolute*. London: Thames & Hudson.
Golitzin, Alexander. 2002. 'A Testimony to Christianity as Transfiguration: The Macarian Homilies and Orthodox Spirituality', in *Orthodox and Wesleyan Spirituality*, ed. S. T. Kimbrough, pp. 129–56. New York: St Vladimir's Seminary Press.
Gombrich, E. H. 1995. *The Story of Art*. London: Phaidon.
Gorbunova-Lomax, Irina. 2018. *The Icon: Truth and Fables*. Brussels: Brussels Academy of Icon Painting.
Gregorios, Paulos. 1980. *The Human Presence: An Orthodox View of Nature*. Madras: Christian Literature Society.
Gregory the Great. 1986. 'Letter to Serenus of Massilia', in *Early Medieval Art, 300–1150: Sources and Document*, trans. Caecilia Davis-Weyer, pp. 47–8. Toronto: University of Toronto Press.
—2004. *The Letters of Gregory the Great*, 3 vols, trans. John R. C. Martyn. Toronto: Pontifical Institute of Mediaeval Studies.
Ham, Jack (ed.). 1995. *Matisse on Art*. Berkeley: University of California Press.
Hart, Aidan. 2022. *Festal Icons*. Leominster: Gracewing.
Heal, Felicity. 2005. *Reformation in Britain and Ireland*. Oxford: Oxford University Press.
Hesychius of Jerusalem. 1963. 'Texts on Sobriety and Prayer, for the Saving of the Soul', in *Writings from the Philokalia: On Prayer of the Heart*, trans. E. Kadloubovsky and Gerald E. H. Palmer, pp. 277–321. London: Faber & Faber.
Hughes, Robert. 1991. *Shock of the New: Art and the Century of Change*. London: Thames & Hudson.
Irenaeus. 1969. *Adversus Haereses* in *The Early Christian Fathers*, trans. Henry Bettenson, pp. 89–140. Oxford: Oxford University Press.
Isaiah the Solitary. 1979. 'On Guarding the Intellect', in *The Philokalia* vol. 1: 8–17.

John of Damascus. 2003. *Three Treatises on the Divine Images*, trans. Andrew Louth. Crestwood: St Vladimir's Seminary Press.

— 2022. *On the Orthodox Faith*, trans. Norman Russell. New York: St Vladimir's Seminary Press

Justiniano, Silouan. 2017. 'Imagination, Expression, Icon: Reclaiming the Internal Prototype', *Orthodox Arts Journal*. https://orthodox-artsjournal.org/imagination-expression-icon-reclaiming-internal-prototype/

Kandinksy, Wassily. 1977. *Concerning the Spiritual in Art*, trans. M. T. H. Sadler. New York: Dover Publications.

Kitzinger, Ernst. 2002, 2003. *Studies in Late Antique, Byzantine and Medieval Western Art*, 2 vols. London: Pindar Press.

Kordis, George. 2018. *The Icon as Communion*, trans. Caroline Makropoulos. Boston: Holy Cross.

Lane, Anthony N. S. 1991. *John Calvin Student of Church Fathers*. London: Bloomsbury Publishing.

Lazarev, Viktor. 1995. *Studies in Byzantine Painting*. London: Pindar Press.

— 2001. *Studies in Early Russian Art*. London: Pindar Press

Lossky, Vladimir. 1957. *The Mystical Theology of the Eastern Church*. London: James Clarkep.

Louth, Andrew. 1996. 'Orthodoxy and Art', in *Living Orthodoxy on the Modern World*, ed. Andrew Walker and Costa Carras, pp. 159–77. London: SPCK.

Luther, Martin. 1997. *Works of Martin Luther*, vol. 6, trans. P. Z. Strodach. Albany, OR: Books for the Ages. https://media.sabda.org/alkitab-8/LIBRARY/LUT_WRK6.PDF

Maguire, Henry. 2021. *Nectar and Illusion: Nature in Byzantine Art and Literature*. Oxford: Oxford University Press.

Mango, Cyril. 1977. 'Historical Introduction', in *Iconoclasm*, ed. Anthony Bryer and Judith Herrin, pp. 1–6. Birmingham: Centre for Byzantine Studies.

Marsengill, Katherine. 2013. *Portraits and Icons: Between Reality and Spirituality in Byzantine Art*. Turnhout: Brepols.

Maximus the Confessor. *Various Texts on Theology, the Divine Economy, and Virtue and Vice*, in *The Philokalia*, vol. 2: 164–284.

— 2014. *On Difficulties in the Church Fathers*, 2 vols, trans. Nicholas Constas. Cambridge, MA: Harvard University Press.

Meyendorff, John. 2010. *A Study of Gregory Palamas*, trans. George Lawrence. New York: St Vladimir's Seminary Press.

Nelson, Robert. 2007. *Spirit of Secular Art: A History of the Sacramental Roots of Contemporary Artistic Values*. Victoria: Monash University

Bibliography

ePress. https://doi.org/10.26180/5f3c6c902501e

Ouspensky, Leonid. 1992. *The Theology of the Icon*. New York: St Vladimir's Seminary Press.

— and Vladimir Lossky. 1997 [1952]. *The Meaning of Icons*. New York: St Vladimir's Seminary Press.

Payton, James R. Jr. 1997. 'Calvin and the Libri Carolini', *The Sixteenth Century* 28/2: 467–80.

Pentcheva, Bissera V. 2010. *The Sensual Icon: Space, Ritual, and the Senses in Byzantium*. Pennsylvania: Pennsylvania State University Press.

— 2017. *Hagia Sophia: Sound, Space, and Spirit in Byzantium*. Pennsylvania: Pennsylvania State University Press.

Peppard, Michael. 2016. *The World's Oldest Church*. New Haven: Yale University Press.

The Philokalia, vol. 1 (1979), vol. 2 (1981), vol. 4 (1995), trans. Gerald E. H. Palmer, Philip Sherrard, and Kallistos Ware. London: Faber & Faber.

Sahas, Daniel. 1986. *Icon and Logos: Sources in Eighth-Century Iconoclasm* (An annotated translation of the Sixth Session of the Seventh Ecumenical Council). Toronto: University of Toronto Press.

Second Vatican Council. 1963. *Sacrosanctum Concilium*. https://www.vatican.va/archive/hist_councils/ii_vatican_council/documents/vat-ii_const_19631204_sacrosanctum-concilium_en.html

The Seven Ecumenical Councils, ed. Philip Schaff and Henry Wace, trans. Henry Percival. 1900. Nicene and Post-Nicene Fathers, series 2, vol. 14. Edinburgh: T. & T. Clark. https://www.documentacatholicaomnia.eu/03d/1819-1893,_Schaff._Philip,_3_Vol_14_The_Seven_Ecumenical_Councils,_EN.pdf

Sherrard, Philip. 1990. *The Sacred in Life and Art*. Ipswich: Golgonooza Press.

— 1992. *Human Image: World Image*. Ipswich: Golgonooza Press.

— 2015. *The Rape of Man and Nature: An Enquiry into the Origins and Consequences of Modern Science*. Evia: Denise Harvey.

Spelman, Leslie P. 1951. 'Luther and the Arts', *The Journal of Aesthetics and Art Criticism* 10/2: 166–75.

Spier, Jeffrey. 2009. In *Picturing the Bible: The Earliest Christian Art*. New Haven: Yale University Press.

Spraggon, Julie. 2003. *Puritan Iconoclasm during the English Civil War*. Woodbridge: Boydell & Brewer.

Stella, Francesco. 2022. 'The Carolingian Answer to the Iconoclastic War and the Birth of Western Art', *European Review* 30: 33–46.

Stjerna, Kirsi I. (ed.). 2015. 'Against the Heavenly Prophets in the Matter of Images and Sacraments, 1525', in *The Annotated Luther: Word and Faith.*, vol. 2, pp. 39–126. Minneapolis: Fortress Press.

Theodore the Studite. 1981. *On the Holy Icons*, trans. Catharine Roth. New York: St Vladimir's Seminary Press.

Tsakiridou, Cornelia E. 2013. *Icons in Time, Persons in Eternity: Orthodox Theology and the Aesthetics of the Christian Image.* New York: Ashgate.

—2019. *Tradition and Transformation in Christian Art: The Transcultural Icon.* New York: Routledge.

Vasari, Giorgio. 1998. *The Lives of the Artists*, trans. Julia Conaway Bondanella, and Peter Bondanella. Oxford: Oxford University Press.

Visel, Jeana. 2016. *Icons in the Western Church.* Minnesota: Liturgical Press.

Wagner, Roger, and Andrew Biggs. 2016. *The Penultimate Curiosity: How Science Swims in the Slipstream of Ultimate Questions.* Oxford: Oxford University Press.

Wallace, Peter. 2014. *The Long European Reformation: Religion, Political Conflict, and the Search for Conformity, 1350–1750.* Basingstoke: Palgrave Macmillan.

Weitzmann, Kurt. 1973. *The Monastery of Saint Catherine on Mount Sinai*, vol. 1, *The Church and Fortress of Justinian.* Ann Arbor: University of Michigan Press

—1976. *The Monastery of Saint Catherine on Mount Sinai*, vol. 2, *The Icons.* Princeton: Princeton University Press.

www.ingramcontent.com/pod-product-compliance
Ingram Content Group UK Ltd.
Pitfield, Milton Keynes, MK11 3LW, UK
UKHW041904230126
10288UKWH00018B/164